3

FASCISM AND THE
INDUSTRIAL LEADERSHIP IN ITALY
1919-1940

Fascism and the Industrial Leadership in Italy, 1919-1940

A Study
in the Expansion
of Private Power under
Fascism

by

ROLAND SARTI

BERKELEY
LOS ANGELES
LONDON
UNIVERSITY OF CALIFORNIA PRESS
1971

University of California Press
Berkeley and Los Angeles, California

University of California Press, Ltd.
London, England

Library of Congress Catalog Card Number: 79-138636
International Standard Book Number: 0-520-01855-9

Printed in the United States of America

To my parents,
FULVIO *and* **PIA**

CONTENTS

ACKNOWLEDGMENTS

Advice, information, constructive criticism, and financial assistance have come from many quarters. Above all, I am indebted to my friend and former mentor John M. Cammett, formerly of Rutgers University and now Dean of the John Jay College of Criminal Justice of the City University of New York, who guided me with his knowledge, enthusiasm, and human warmth through an earlier version of this study that was accepted as my doctoral dissertation by Rutgers University in 1967. In the Rutgers Department of History, I am also indebted to professors Trajan Stoianovich, Warren I. Susman, and Henry R. Winkler who read and criticized the dissertation. A word of thanks also goes to my colleagues on the Columbia University Seminar on Modern Italy who have heard and commented on parts of this manuscript.

Dr. Giuseppe Cardillo, who directs the *Istituto Italiano di Cultura* in New York City, was kind enough to provide me with letters of introduction that greatly facilitated my work in Italy. Drs. Costanzo Casucci, Renato Grispo, Guido Guerra, and Director Leopoldo Sandri, all from the *Archivio Centrale dello Stato* in Rome, were most helpful in introducing me to useful archival material. Professors Renzo De Felice of the University of Salerno and Rosario

Romeo of the University of Rome were kind enough to take an interest in this project and direct me in the difficult task of locating some of the documentation. Miss Cipriana Scelba, head of the American Commission for Cultural Exchanges with Italy, frequently took time out of her busy schedule to give me the benefit of her deep knowledge of Italian academic circles and administrative channels.

Of the people who had a direct personal knowledge of the events discussed in this study, the most helpful were former Senator Ettore Conti and former minister of finance Alberto De Stefani. Their comments and reminiscences have given me an appreciation of the problems and personalities of the period that I could not have gained through the written evidence alone. The late Ernesto Rossi, a luminous figure in the Italian resistance to fascism, was most generous with advice and encouragement. Dr. Pietro Grifone, who was also an active anti-Fascist, supplied me with useful information based on his thorough knowledge of Italian industry during the Fascist period.

A number of institutions have also been most cooperative. This study would have been either impossible or incomplete without the resources and courtesies extended by the New York Public Library, the _Biblioteca Nazionale,_ the _Biblioteca di Storia Contemporanea,_ the _Biblioteca della Camera dei Deputati,_ the _Biblioteca Alessandrina,_ and the Library of the _Confederazione Generale dell'Industria Italiana,_ all in Rome. The United States Steel Foundation offered a U. S. Steel Fellowship (1962-1964) and the United States Government a Fulbright Fellowship to Italy (1964-1965). Finally, I gratefully acknowledge the cooperation of the Department of History of the University of Massachusetts in giving me the opportunity to complete this manuscript.

A special word of appreciation goes to my wife, Rose, who has shared all my burdens and apprehensions through years of research and writing.

ABBREVIATIONS

ASIA *Associazione fra le Società Italiane per Azioni* (Association of Italian Joint Stock Companies).

Atti. Camera *Atti del Parlamento Italiano. Camera dei Deputati.* Official minutes of the debates in the Italian Chamber of Deputies.

Atti. Senato *Atti del Parlamento Italiano. Camera dei Senatori.* Official minutes of the debates in the Italian Senate.

CGII *Confederazione Generale dell'Industria Italiana* (General Confederation of Italian Industry).

O. I. *L'Organizzazione Industriale.* Journal published by the CGII.

Opera Omnia *Opera Omnia di Benito Mussolini,* ed. by Edoardo and Duilio Susmel (36 vols.; Florence: La Fenice, 1951-1963).

Riv. Pol. Econ. Rivista di Politica Economica. Monthly review published by the ASIA and CGII.

Riv. Soc. Comm. Rivista delle Società Commerciali. Forerunner of the *Riv. Pol. Econ.*

INTRODUCTION

The fox knows many tricks,
the hedgehog only one. A good one.
(Archilochos, *Proverb for a Great Scoundrel*)

The industrial leadership of Italy dealt with fascism as the hedge-hog deals with the fox. The Italian industrialists pursued a clear and simple goal with tenacity and determination. While the Fascists dispersed their energies in the pursuit of multiple and often conflict-ing goals, the industrialists concentrated on retaining maximum independence in the management of their enterprises and trade as-sociations. They held that these establishments were the source of their economic power which no government could ignore, and that managerial independence and organizational autonomy were close-ly related. Their vast network of trade associations—which we will call "organized industry"—gave them the political leverage to counterbalance the influence of self-styled social revolutionaries within the Fascist party.

The self-styled revolutionaries, and the political instability they imparted to the Fascist movement, preoccupied the industrial leaders. Unlike many anti-Fascists who called fascism a socially con-servative or even reactionary phenomenon, the industrialists never took Fascist conservatism for granted. And, because they never took that conservatism for granted, they were able, with the help of other vested interests like the monarchy, the Church, the army, and the civil service, to prolong the life of the existing social system with minimum change. Fascist reforms attenuated the traditional distinction between the public and private sectors of society. This transformation, however, was generally acceptable and, indeed, advantageous to the business leadership. By the Second World War, the industrialists were more entrenched in the economic and social system than they were when fascism came to power.

The industrialists looked upon political activity in a purely instrumental way. Politics was a means of keeping the government on the path of economic and social orthodoxy. Because they prided themselves on their political pragmatism, they approached fascism without ideological preconceptions. Although some industrialists expressed reservations about the style and content of Fascist politics, most were attracted by the movement's responsiveness to outside pressures and, above all, by Mussolini's political craftsmanship.

In its formative stage, fascism defied classification according to the traditional canons of politics; it lacked internal cohesion; it was a conglomerate of groups and ideas drawn from the entire political spectrum, ranging from the rigidly conservative to the impulsively revolutionary. There were always many fascisms in Italy and every man could choose the one he liked. The lack of discipline and cohesion led many industrialists and allegedly shrewd politicians to believe that, once in power, fascism would gradually dissolve into the mainstream of traditional liberal politics. The industrialists accepted fascism before the March on Rome with the expectation that it would not remain the revolutionary movement it claimed to be.

Mussolini was the logical leader of the movement because he was sufficiently flexible and opportunistic to deal with and manipulate the most dissimilar elements both inside and outside the movement. Through Mussolini the industrialists planned to exert leverage on the movement as a whole. His reasonableness and apparent receptivity to their demands led them to believe that he was willing and, with their support and encouragement, able to restrain the more turbulent and revolutionary Fascists. Mussolini, who relished the role of compromiser and mediator because, ultimately, it made everyone dependent upon him, was careful not to disillusion the industrialists.

For the purpose of our study we have described fascism without its totalitarian connotations. We must now identify the group which we call the "industrial leadership," the "business leadership," or more generally, the "industrialists." These three terms interchangeably refer to a relatively small group of leading personalities who held office or were active in the country's two most influential business pressure groups: the *Confederazione Generale dell'Industria Italiana* (CGII), generally known in Italy as *Confindustria*, and the *Associazione fra le Società Italiane per Azioni* (ASIA). Their constituencies overlapped to such an extent that they are best considered as one. Although the ASIA extended membership to all business corporations and included many bankers and financiers, it was dominated by industrialists. When the industrialists organized themselves separately in the CGII, they took effective steps to make sure that the two organizations would work in unison.

There are both advantages and disadvantages to making the ASIA and CGII the focus of our study. The most serious disadvantage of concentrating on the activities of these two top associations is the danger of losing sight of the demands of particular business groups, personal relationships, and individuals whose actions affect the outcome of any historical process. However, our organizational approach is deliberate and was chosen in the belief that organized industry's accomplishments were more significant than those of the most powerful businessmen acting as individuals. Personalities are considered only when their actions illuminate the collective role of business in the evolution of Fascist society.

We will not show how individual businessmen may have gained influence because of their personal contacts with Fascist leaders. Personal favoritism exists in every known political system, and the fact that it existed under fascism tells us nothing of historical value about the Fascist experience. By concentrating on the collective behavior of business we can learn about the decision-making process in Fascist Italy. The ASIA and CGII are an ideal focus for our study because they were designed to operate at high political levels in the general interests of private initiative rather than for the particular interests of individual firms or narrow interest groups.

By studying their activities we will be able to survey the evolution of the Fascist state.

The CGII was the more influential and prestigious of the two organizations. When the Fascists made their successful bid for power in October 1922, the CGII was the most powerful private pressure group in the country. There were few opposing forces. Organized labor had suffered crippling defeats for which the CGII and the Fascists were jointly responsible. Socialists and Communists were busy quarreling among themselves, unable to work out a common strategy against fascism. The Church had not yet settled their differences with the government that were part of the legacy of the *Risorgimento*. In contrast, the CGII was capably led by industrialists who felt industry was denied political influence commensurate to its economic power. In Italy, where most private pressure groups were just beginning to organize, the industrialists enjoyed an important advantage at the moment when the political future of the country hung in the balance.

The Fascist takeover transformed the CGII from a powerful private pressure group into an even more powerful branch of the public bureaucracy. Until then, the CGII had resembled the National Association of Manufacturers in the United States. In the process of creating the corporative state, fascism recognized the CGII as the official and sole representative of all industrial employers vis-à-vis the government and the labor unions. In this new capacity, the CGII enjoyed the autonomy of a private pressure group and the powers of a public agency. The directives issued by the CGII after the official recognition were legally binding on all industrial employers, particularly with regard to labor negotiations. Although the industrial leaders were given extensive powers over the rank-and-file, fascism imposed public regulation on the CGII in name only.

Fascism enabled the industrialists to forge a chain of command that eventually reached from the CGII to the smallest firms. Because of that chain of command, the leadership of the CGII can indeed be called the industrial leadership. And because no other business association equalled the CGII's political influence during the Fascist period, we are also justified calling it the business leadership.

In dealing with the industrial leadership, fascism was tactful without being subservient. The dialogue between the Fascist and the industrial leaders developed according to certain ground rules. The industrialists were suspicious of Fascist revolutionary syndicalists like labor leader Edmondo Rossoni who seemed determined to radicalize the regime. Although the industrialists opposed these Fascist radicals openly, they kept their opposition within definite limits. To go beyond the limits meant risking a break with the regime, a possibility the industrialists were not prepared to face. Consequently, they rarely rejected Fascist proposals for economic and social reform *a priori*. They dissented and debated within acceptable limits by questioning details rather than principles and were thus able to weaken or eliminate specific provisions that threatened entrepreneurial autonomy without incurring the charge of ideological heresy. Neither side was embarrassed by risky open confrontations. The corporative state, with all its ambiguities and weaknesses, was largely the product of this continual give and take between the Fascist and the industrial leaders.

The industrialists' strategy worked because both sides showed amazing flexibility. Although fascism claimed to be monolithic and totalitarian, it was really a most accommodating political regime. It carried on the practice of *trasformismo* which was well-rooted in Italian politics before fascism came to power. The industrialists were more interested in the details of economic and social policy than in the grand lines of political conduct. Their influence on foreign policy was always limited and they were not too unhappy with this arrangement. Their aloofness from purely political issues paid off when the regime collapsed. The political purge which followed World War II had few repercussions in entrepreneurial and managerial circles. At that point, the hedgehog reaped the reward of its political obscurity.

The absence of ideological debate was one of the characteristics of *trasformismo* before and during fascism. Decisions were often reached on the basis of informal contacts and personal understandings. The result was a "clientelism" strongly reminiscent of a feudal society. Therefore, the industrial leadership had to be chosen among those industrialists who enjoyed good personal relations with the Fascist leadership in general and with Mussolini in particular. Gino Olivetti (no relation to the manufacturers of business machines) was the one exception; he had to resign as secretary of the CGII at the end of 1933, mainly because of the strong personal enmities he aroused in Fascist circles. That he lasted at his post long after fascism had come to power is a good indicator of the industrialists' independence under the Fascist regime.

Political invisibility was a valuable asset for any industrialist aspiring to political influence. A good example of the unobtrusive but politically influential industrialist was Antonio Stefano Benni, a manufacturer of mechanical appliances who was president of the CGII from 1923 to 1934. His low keyed personality and self-effacing manner disguised exceptional political and organizational talents. He owed his long tenure as president of the CGII and his considerable influence in the Chamber of Deputies to which he was elected in 1921 to the respect he inspired in Mussolini. Like many of his industrial colleagues, Benni was disdainful of gesture and rhetoric. How he and his colleagues developed a good working relationship with the most rhetoric-prone and histrionic contemporary political movement is a paradox that requires explanation.

The explanation must begin with an assessment of the relative strength of fascism and organized industry between 1919 and 1922 when both fascism and the CGII became forces to be reckoned with. Opponents of the regime rumored persistently that under fascism the CGII was a state within the state. The rumors find architectural confirmation in the physical layout of *Piazza Venezia* at the center of the city, the symbolic heart of the regime. In 1920 the directors of the CGII decided to locate their main offices in a modern facsimile of *Palazzo Venezia* located directly across the square from the famous Renaissance palace. Some years later, when Mussolini decided to move his headquarters into *Palazzo Venezia,* the country's business and political leaderships found themselves housed in similar fortress-like structures on opposite sides of the same square. The architectural scene, dominated by the white marble monument to Victor Emmanuel II, so familiar to tourists, provides a commentary in stone and concrete on the historical problem discussed here.

I

FASCISM AND THE
INDUSTRIAL LEADERSHIP IN ITALY
FROM 1919 TO THE MARCH ON ROME

Italian industrialists have always felt politically vulnerable. Confronted, in the course of history, by economically conservative and politically influential agricultural interests, aggressive labor unions, strong political parties ideologically committed to the liquidation of capitalism, and governments responsive to a variety of pressures, Italian industrialists developed a sacrificial-lamb-complex. In Benni's words, they were ". . . Daniels in the lion's den." [1] Their sense of frustration was understandable. While entrepreneurs in the more advanced Western nations were able to face the pressures one by one, or over a span of several generations, Italian industrialists had to deal with them simultaneously. That is the price paid by latecomers to the industrial revolution.

Economists point out that the Italian economy reached its "take-off" stage during the first decade of the twentieth century. With few exceptions, the psychology of Italian entrepreneurs lagged be-

---

[1] *Atti. Camera,* 1924–1926, V, 4934.

hind the economic and technological potential of Italian industry. At a time when employers in Western Europe and America were beginning to accept and welcome the advantages of collective bargaining, Italian employers reacted to labor unions with the gut reaction of first-generation capitalists. They considered membership in a labor union an act of personal betrayal. The good worker was expected to defer to his employer as a benevolent, if somewhat despotic, *pater familias*.[2] The employers projected the values of a pre-industrial, family-oriented society into industrial labor relations.

As a result of this gap between entrepreneurial psychology and the objective conditions of production, employers saw in organized labor and popular unrest politically and socially subversive developments. As a rule, they did not see labor agitations as the symptoms of agricultural and industrial laborers' growing desire to obtain a greater share of the economic benefits provided by the existing system of production. The unnecessarily bloody repression of the riots that broke out in Italy in 1898 was indicative of an exaggerated fear of social revolution among the economic and the political leadership.

Shortly thereafter more modern ideas began to circulate among government officials and in entrepreneurial circles. Under Premier Giovanni Giolitti, the government became a neutral and impartial third party in labor conflicts. The police and the army no longer played the role of class militias. With the emergence of new industries and the expansion of older ones, a new industrial leadership appeared. Foreign capital and personnel brought new ideas from across the Alps. German and Swiss industrialists helped to develop the vast hydroelectric potential of Piedmont and Lombardy. French influences were particularly strong in the rapidly developing automobile industry of Turin. But Italian entrepreneurs were also active. During the first decade of this century these leading representatives of the new industries were active in the establishment of industrial trade and regional organizations: Carlo Esterle and Ettore Conti in the electrical industry, Emilio De Benedetti, Giuseppe Mazzini (no relation to the nineteenth-century

---

[2] Louis Bonnefon-Craponne, *L'Italie au travail* (Paris: Pierre Roger, 1916), p. 26.

patriot), and Giovanni Silvestri in the mechanical industry, Guido Donegani in chemicals, Giovanni Agnelli of Fiat, and the Pirelli family in rubber and electrical power cables.[3]

Self-confidence and political ambition characterized the new entrepreneurs. They were open to new ideas. A few, like Ettore Conti, even recognized the legitimacy and advantages of collective bargaining, although as a group they were convinced that the needs of production must take precedence over social reforms. The industrialists saw themselves as the forerunners of a new economic order that would propel the nation into the twentieth century. In Conti's words, the industrialists had to organize in order to wrest their proper share of power from "a political class formed largely of lawyers ignorant of the real needs of the country." [4] According to Conti, Italian culture was too steeped in humanistic rhetoric; it lacked the practical wisdom necessary for survival in the age of technology. In other words, the expertise of the engineer would succeed where the rhetoric of the lawyer had failed.

Thus, among the industrial leaders two distinct strains were converging to produce a single result. On the one hand, there was their exaggerated fear of social revolution which increased their political sensitivity. On the other, there was a new confidence in their technological and managerial skills, and an allegedly superior sense of reality. On both counts, they aspired to carry out a rescue operation that was to restore the social order and to make the government more responsive to the needs of industrial production. In order to fulfill this self-imposed political mission, the leaders of industry needed an organizational network that could mobilize the economic resources of every sector of production in the struggle against allegedly excessive and subversive demands of organized labor, and the unwillingness of liberal governments, especially Giolitti's, to resist popular demands for social reform.

---

[3] Paolo Spriano, *Socialismo e classe operaia a Torino dal 1892 al 1913* (Turin: Giulio Einaudi, 1958), pp. 171–175, 210–219, 245–248. On the origins of industrial associations, see also Mario Abrate, *La lotta sindacale nella industrializzazione in Italia, 1906–1926* (Turin: Franco Angeli, 1967), pp. 31–41, and Rinaldo Rigola, *Storia del movimento operaio italiano* (Milan: Editoriale Domus, 1947), pp. 317–322.

[4] Ettore Conti, *Dal taccuino di un borghese* (Milan: Garzanti, 1946), p. 77.

THE ORGANIZATION OF INDUSTRIAL INTEREST GROUPS BEFORE THE MARCH ON ROME.

The proliferation of industrial pressure groups during the first decade of this century was a direct consequence of the political ambitions of the industrial leadership. Unlike previous trade organizations which had served primarily to regulate production and prices, the new associations had a definite political vocation. The prototype was the Industrial League of Turin, founded in 1906. It led the struggle against organized labor in that city and helped establish similar associations elsewhere in Piedmont. It was the parent association of the Italian Confederation of Industry (1910), which, in turn, was the direct ancestor of the CGII. Also in 1910 in Milan, industrialists and financiers joined forces to establish the ASIA. The industrial leadership that was to play such an important role in Fascist Italy had already asserted itself by the end of the first decade of this century.

The First World War opened new economic and political opportunities for the industrial leadership. Although neither the ASIA nor the Italian Confederation of Industry urged the government to abandon its initial neutrality in the conflict, individual industrial interest groups such a steel producers, armament manufacturers, and shipbuilders were interventionist. The war provided opportunities which all industrialists were quick to seize. Manufacturing and finance drew even closer than they had been before the war to form the giant combines necessary to sustain the war effort. Industrialists and government officials sat side by side on the same planning agencies where they learned to appreciate the advantages of economic planning and cooperation. Never before had the industrialists been so close to the center of political power, so deeply involved in the decision-making process.[5]

---

[5] Federico Chessa, "La concentrazione delle industrie e la Guerra delle Nazioni," *Riv. Soc. Comm.*, IX (October 1919), 724–740. Also, Luigi Gaddi, "Per la riforma della tariffa doganale," *Riv. Pol. Econ.*, XXVI (April 1936), 240–248, and Gino Olivetti, "L'organizzazione sindacale degli industriali in Italia," *O. I.* October 15, 1928, p. 225. All three publications were published by the CGII.

The lessons of economic planning and cooperation were not forgotten when the war ended. As the soldiers brought back from the trenches a new awareness of their collective importance and a determination to obtain redress for grievances past and present, so the businessmen resolved not to relinquish their share of political influence. A new organizational drive touched every sector of the national economy. In December 1918, the directors of ASIA proposed to establish a new nation-wide association of industrial trade organizations. The Italian Confederation of Industry provided the model, but whereas that association functioned only in the "industrial triangle," the area between Turin, Milan, and Genoa, the new confederation was to be national in fact and in name.[6]

The man chiefly responsible for the establishment of CGII was Gino Olivetti, who played a unique role in industry. The fact that he had no major managerial responsibilities of his own in industry enabled him to devote most of his time and seemingly inexhaustible energy to organization and politics. He was the only professional organizer in industry. And since he represented no particular industrial interest, he was also the ideal mediator between rival industrial groups. However, his complete dedication to the cause of business made him a controversial figure in national politics. Hence, he carefully worked through less controversial and more prestigious industrialists capable of giving the new organization a degree of authority unparalleled among business pressure groups. Since the more prestigious figures were already connected with ASIA or the Industrial League of Turin, the CGII had a close connection with both. The first president of CGII was Dante Ferraris, a vice-president of Fiat and president of both ASIA and the Industrial League of Turin.

The organizational enthusiasm was so great that the promoters of CGII even considered the possibility of setting up a super-confederation of employer organizations from agriculture, banking, commerce, and industry. Such a combination might well have

---

[6] On the continuity between the Italian Confederation of Industry and the CGII, see Leo Vidotto, *L'organizzazione industriale lombarda nell'ultimo cinquantennio* (Milan: Industrie Grafiche Italiane Stucchi, 1959), pp. 37, 153–174.

given the capitalists a decisive advantage in their post-war confrontation with organized labor. Fortunately for labor, the project foundered amid obscure rivalries and misunderstandings. Instead of one super-confederation, four separate confederations emerged between December 1918 and April 1919: the General Confederation of Italian Agriculture, the General Confederation of Italian Banking, the General Confederation of Italian Commerce, and the General Confederation of Italian Industry (CGII).[7]

The CGII, inaugurated in Rome on April 8, 1919, quickly surpassed all other confederations in influence and prestige. The reasons for its dominant position are not hard to find. In addition to being run by the most political-minded leaders of the Italian business world, it was supported by the combined resources of industry and finance. Its administrative structure was designed to facilitate the closest collaboration between the two groups. The CGII was divided into two branches, a Syndical Section and an Economic Section; the first designed to deal with organized labor, the second to influence government officials and administrators in the formulation and application of economic policy. The Economic Section grew out of the research staff of ASIA and was an integral part of both organizations.

The arrangement permitted industry and finance to work together on matters of common interest and, at the same time, to preserve a separate identity. A complete identification of the two would not have been desirable. There were critics who objected to the existence of strong ties between industry and finance and who feared that purely financial speculations might vitiate the course of industrial production and there were also strong rivalries and mutual suspicion between individual industrialists and financiers. Various attempts by individual industrialists to gain control of established banking institutions in the immediate post-war period testify to the bad feelings between these two sectors of the national economy. Nevertheless, when it came to trade, tariffs, taxation, gov-

---

[7] The progress of the organizational campaign can be followed in *Corriere della Sera,* February 1, 1919, p. 2; April 3, 1919, p. 4; April 10, 1919, p. 4; Also, *Il Sole,* April 12, 1919, p. 1, and *L'Italia Industriale,* I (July–September 1919), 23. *L'Italia Industriale* was published by the CGII from 1919 to 1921. Copies of its issues are now rare.

ernment spending, and monetary policy there was a sufficiently strong community of interests between industry and finance to make close cooperation mutually advantageous. The Economic Section of CGII made the cooperation possible.[8]

Organizational efficiency was assured by avoiding excessive bureaucratization. The founders of CGII aimed at a balance between a concentration of power in the hands of their elected officials and the decentralization of the decision-making process. Each section had its legislative assembly, its administration and research services. The Syndical Section's executive body, the directive council, assured quick responses in the unpredictable and volatile area of labor relations. The directive council became industry's most authoritative mouthpiece in labor controversies.

The Economic Section successfully collected statistical data on a vast range of economic problems. Because neither the government, nor any private group, was in a position to supply such information, the CGII enjoyed a unique advantage. Its data were passed on to lawmakers and public administrators who used them to formulate and implement policy. Thus, public decisions were based on privately collected evidence, a situation which has not changed in Italy today.[9]

The work of the two sections was coordinated at the top by the general assembly and the executive committee of the CGII. The general assembly consisted of the assemblies of the two sections sitting jointly. As it was a large body and difficult to convene, it met only once a year and issued only the most general directives. The interpretation and execution of the directives rested with the executive committee, a body small enough to permit prompt action.

The executive committee worked under the direct supervision of the president who was elected by the general assembly. His powers were broad enough to accommodate the most ambitious individual. After an initial period when the presidency changed

---

[8] On the initial relationship between the ASIA and CGII, see ASIA, *Relazione sull'opera svolta dall'Associazione nell'anno 1920* (Rome: Bolognesi, 1921), pp. 16–17.

[9] On the internal structure of the CGII, see its *Annuario 1922* (Rome: La Poligrafica Nazionale, 1922), pp. 84–91, and *Annuario 1923* (Rome: Cooperativa Tipografica Egeria, 1923), pp. 105–106.

hands at brief intervals (from 1919 to 1923 five different industrialists held the post), the presidency became an authoritative, long-term position. Antonio Stefano Benni held the post from January 1923 to January 1934. After an interim period of ten months, when Alberto Pirelli was acting president, the office went to Giuseppe Volpi, a shrewd businessman connected with many enterprises who was particularly identified with the electrical industry, who retained it until May 1943. The personalities of these three men were quite different but they all had political ambition, felt at home in business and in political circles, and were personally close to Mussolini.

A special word must be said about the office of secretary-general and about Gino Olivetti who held it from 1919 to 1934. Although the president was officially the first in command, the secretary wielded greater power. This can be attributed not so much to the office itself as to Gino Olivetti's personality. Politically ambitious, a polished public speaker, thoroughly familiar with the problems of Italian industry, persistent and resourceful, Olivetti was the logical choice for the post of secretary. He had the ability and the disposition to defend the interests of private industry with single-minded devotion both as secretary of the CGII and as a member of the Chamber of Deputies to which he was elected in 1919 through the backing of Turinese industrialists.

Olivetti's attitude toward fascism was complex. Although he approved of the Fascist commitment to law, order, and discipline which had restored the unquestioned authority of the employer within the factory, he also feared the revolutionary potential of certain currents of Fascist thought. He was particularly outspoken against advocates of the Fascist corporative state because he saw in corporativism a threat to entrepreneurial autonomy. Mussolini, who did not like stubborn critics even when they were as diplomatic as Olivetti, took an immediate dislike to the man. In 1922, he resentfully referred to Olivetti as "the *duce* of Italian industry." [10] When the corporative reform was finally enacted in 1934 over Olivetti's opposition, Mussolini forced his resignation as secretary-general of the CGII. Olivetti, a Jew, was subsequently

---

[10] *Opera Omnia*, XVIII, 44.

forced into exile by the racial laws of 1938. He died in 1942 in Argentina, a bitter and disillusioned man.[11]

Above the legislative and executive agencies of the CGII was the shadow cabinet of the Central Industrial Committee, a body that is not mentioned in the CGII's charter or in any formal document. Its official status is impossible to define, although it seems it was the ultimate decision-making body for both the ASIA and CGII. Its membership varied from time to time but usually was around twenty members, drawn from the presidential staffs of the two organizations. It kept no records, issued few statements, and made rare public appearances. There is no way of documenting its activities. It is mentioned here because its existence, and the vast official and unofficial powers vested in the president and secretary-general, indicate that the government of CGII was designed to concentrate power in the hands of a few influential industrialists.[12]

Seats in the CGII's general assembly were apportioned by an intricate formula that took into account the size of the labor force and the amount of invested capital represented by each member. There is no need to go into the complexities of the system to see that it was designed to give the greatest political weight to the economically more powerful interests. Small producers were systematically discriminated against. Their resentments found expression in several unsuccessful attempts made between 1919 and 1925 to create independent organizations of small and medium industry. Olivetti complained frequently about the alleged individualism of Italian producers who looked upon membership in an industrial association as an intolerable restriction of their freedom of action.

The directors of CGII always proclaimed scrupulous respect for the rights of individual firms and industrial associations and rarely intervened in the internal affairs of particular firms. Membership was never extended to firms or individuals, only to industrial associations. Members were allowed to settle their own problems unless the issues at stake touched the general interests of industry. If this

---

[11] Olivetti's attitude toward fascism is discussed briefly in Abrate, *La lotta sindacale,* pp. 455–460.

[12] Felice Guarneri, *Battaglie economiche tra le due grandi guerre* (Milan: Garzanti, 1953), I, 7. Guarneri headed the economic and statistical services of the CGII from 1920 to 1935.

was the case, and it was many times, CGII's officials used both the carrot and the stick to enforce compliance with their decisions.

Although strong-arm tactics were used only as a last resort, they could never be ruled out. The textile industry provides a case in point. Leading textile personalities like Giorgio Mylius, Giuseppe Riva, Raimondo Targetti, and Carlo Tarlarini played important roles in the initial years of the CGII's life. Targetti was even elected to its presidency in 1921. But a serious internal split developed during the debate over the new tariff law of July 1921, when the CGII came out in favor of a strong protectionist tariff. Steel, machinery, chemicals, and sugar refining were enthusiastically protectionist. These sectors had expanded at an abnormally fast pace during the war and were now in serious difficulties. To them, protectionism was an economic panacea.

Textile producers, on the other hand, did not wish to provoke retaliation from abroad by raising tariffs. They were adequately protected under the old tariff law of 1887 and were well established on foreign markets. Higher tariffs were likely to hurt their export business. By supporting a protective system that was even more rigid than the one introduced in July 1921, the CGII revealed a definite bias in favor of heavy industry that caused more friction between light and heavy industry in years to come. In time, light industry was relegated to second-class citizenship within the CGII.

We can now sum up the situation within organized industry before the March on Rome. The CGII was already a power to be reckoned with without any help from the Fascists. It represented 144 industrial associations located in every region of the country except the industrially undeveloped regions of Basilicata and Calabria. Its chain of command covered a vast network of national and regional trade federations and multi-trade employer associations at the provincial level. At the same time, the CGII was far from having complete control over the representation of industrial employers. Small producers and craftsmen were still unorganized. Internal discipline was shaky. In 1922 a number of firms refused to pay the double membership fees, one to the provincial association and one to the national trade federation as required by CGII regulations.[13]

---

[13] CGII, *Annuario 1922*, pp. 81–84.

Considerations of organizational convenience influenced the attitude of industrial leaders toward fascism. In their dealings with organized labor and individual employers, the industrial leaders stressed the importance of hierarchy, discipline, and subordination. They were therefore psychologically ready to accept the Fascist concept of leadership which stressed the same principles. Because fascism asserted that every individual must acknowledge and fulfill his obligations to a superior authority, its rise to power could create an authoritarian climate that would hasten the fulfillment of the industrialists' organizational goals.

At the same time, the industrialists could not fully identify with fascism because there was always the possibility that an energetic though perhaps confused revolutionary Fascist government might threaten the independence of organized industry. This lingering fear explains why in their relations with outside groups the industrial leaders often emphasized respect for freedom of initiative and association. Their attitude could be both liberal and authoritarian, depending on circumstances. Aware of the existence of serious contradictions in their thinking, the industrialists thought of themselves as pragmatists who reject absolute principles and logical abstractions. The Fascists struck precisely the same pose for the same reason. The presence of these contradictions explains the peculiar love-hate relationship that developed between the industrial and the Fascist leadership before the March on Rome. For a more complete explanation we must turn to the political context in which that relationship developed.

THE INDUSTRIALISTS IN POLITICS

The CGII was born with an unmistakable political vocation. Although the industrialists preferred to avoid publicity, political concerns were uppermost in their thought. Ettore Conti, who was elected president of the CGII in June 1920, wrote in his diary that the CGII was designed to act as a "showcase" in which industry would display its best men "with an eye on their future participation in government." [14] Dante Ferraris, the CGII's first president, was even more explicit in his inaugural address of April 10, 1919:

---

[14] Conti, *Dal taccuino di un borghese,* p. 229.

Scattered until now into usually autonomous organizations, the industrialists have not asserted themselves as a ruling class. They have fought for the future of their industries on economic grounds [but] they have been absent from public life as a tightly organized group with an active and united leadership. New times now summon the industrialists to play a larger role in public affairs.[15]

Military victory had aroused great expectations in Italian society and the industrialists were no exception. Their political position at the end of the war can be summed up briefly: eagerness to exploit all possibilities for economic expansion abroad, and impatience to abolish all wartime government controls over business and production. They were to be disappointed on both counts. Disappointment with the course of the peace negotiations at Versailles convinced the industrialists that Italy had won the war only to lose the peace. They took up Gabriele d'Annunzio's cry about the "mutilated victory" and played it for all it was worth. The theme appeared in Ferraris' inaugural speech when he urged the country to "gather all its energies and look after its own interests before the enemies of yesterday and today unite against us and make it impossible for us to settle our problems." [16]

The problems to which Ferraris referred were serious enough. The most serious obstacle to the continuation of production immediately after the war was a critical shortage of coal and raw materials. Given their natural scarcity at home, the solution had to be found abroad. The industrialists were willing to capitalize on the country's position as a victorious power. They supported the controversial project to establish an Italian sphere of influence in the Turkish region of Adalia because that part of Turkey was reputed to be rich in coal.[17]

To speed up the flow of industrial supplies, they urged the government to abolish all wartime restrictions on imports and to exact the strictest observance of Italian requests for compensations in raw

---

15 *Riv. Soc. Comm.*, IX (April 1919), p. 286.

16 *Ibid.*, p. 288. On the industrialists' tendency to blame domestic unrest on the unfavorable course of the peace negotiations, see ASIA, *Relazione sull'opera svolta dall'Associazione nell'anno 1919* (Rome: Officina Tipografica Bodoni, 1920), pp. 3–4.

17 *Riv. Soc. Comm.*, IX (April 1919), 286–287.

materials from Austria and Germany.[18] Their stand against import restrictions was also a political ploy to allay popular discontent over the scarcity of vital food supplies and did not signify a reversal of the CGII's protectionist policy.

The most dramatic expression of industry's interest in economic expansion abroad occurred in February 1920 when Ettore Conti led a warship and a detachment of Italian marines to the Russian regions of Armenia, Georgia, and Azerbaijan in the hope that these regions' chaotic internal situations might offer opportunities for Italian commercial penetration. Mussolini was supposed to join the expedition as an observer but backed out at the last moment for reasons that are not entirely clear.[19]

Mussolini's interest in the expedition underscores the similarity between the industrial and Fascist view of foreign policy. Both stood on the same side of the basic political division in Italy: they defended the decision to enter the war and were decidedly nationalistic when it came to the peace settlement. They charged that the political leadership was too accommodating toward the country's wartime allies and that it was not sufficiently determined to obtain adequate economic, political, and territorial compensations at the peace conference. Neutralists and all those who favored a soft peace were dismissed as misguided utopians or treasonous enemies of the state. It was one of the anomalies of the Italian political scene that the controversy between neutralists and interventionists was even more bitter after the war than it had been before.

It can be argued that the similarity between industry and fascism was only skin deep because the industrialists thought only in terms of economic expansion while the Fascists were avowed political imperialists and territorial annexationists. No doubt there were differences of degree and motivation between them, but the differences were less important in the long run than the similarities. Being on the same side of the great political debate in the postwar period facilitated agreement on other matters. It was a prerequisite, not a sufficient cause, for the closer understanding on purely domestic issues that developed eventually.

---

[18] *Corriere della Sera,* June 8, 1919, p. 5.
[19] Conti, *Dal taccuino di un borghese,* p. 99.

In discussing the relationship between the industrial leadership and fascism, careful distinctions of time, place, and degree of involvement must be made. The turning point occurred during the second half of 1920, and coincided closely with the workers' unsuccessful occupation of the factories of September 1920. The workers' forcible eviction of employers from the factories and their short-lived attempt to run the factories without the cooperation of capital and management marked the high point of the revolutionary wave in postwar Italy. It also marked the beginning of the anti-Socialist, anti-labor reaction that became the joint enterprise of the industrial and the Fascist leadership.

Until 1920 the industrialists had only a passing interest in fascism. Fascism was still only one of several super-nationalistic groups active in the country. It was the brainchild of one man—Benito Mussolini—and its sparse following was limited to the major industrial cities of the north. Mussolini had friends and sympathizers in industrial circles. Giovanni Agnelli, Carlo Esterle, Mario and Pio Perrone (the two brothers who ran the vast Ansaldo industrial complex), had provided financial support for Mussolini's newspaper *Il Popolo d'Italia* as early as 1914. The reason for this support was probably a desire to weaken the Socialist party by providing a public forum for its most well-known and articulate heretic.[20] It is interesting to note that Dante Ferraris was the only member of Francesco Saverio Nitti's government of June 1919 who was spared Mussolini's blistering criticism. Nitti and his supporters were denounced by the Fascists as the personifications of bourgeois timidity, pacifism, and lack of nationalistic fervor. Ferraris, however, was described as a self-made "man of action with a solid and constructive mind." [21]

As for Mussolini, the industrialists were a useful source of badly needed funds. Venality was not one of Mussolini's weaknesses but, practical politician that he was, he understood the importance of money for political success. And the industrialists contributed, al-

---

[20] Brunello Vigezzi, *L'Italia di fronte alla prima guerra mondiale. I. L'Italia neutrale* (Milan–Naples: Riccardo Ricciardi, 1966), pp. 365, 646–647, 661–663, 949.

[21] *Il Popolo d'Italia*, June 24, 1919, p. 1. Also, Nitti's introduction to Enrico Flores, *Eredità di guerra* (Rome: Edizioni di Politica, 1947), p. 31.

though probably not as much as the landowners of the Po Valley who resented the power of Socialist agricultural labor unions and cooperatives.[22] The financial ties may have been responsible for some rumors current at the time. The Florentine *squadrista* Umberto Banchelli, an important figure in the early Fascist movement, referred to Mussolini as "a rash and stubborn politician perhaps too closely tied to industrial interests." [23]

If taken at face value, Banchelli's description of Mussolini is misleading. Mussolini was not averse to cultivating prominent industrialists, provided he could do so without making compromising political commitments. While he accepted their money, he also protected his freedom of action. His eventual turn in the direction of big business was motivated by political considerations, not by a financial calculus. To Mussolini the industrialists were only one pawn to be manipulated in a subtle political game.

Mussolini's actions must be seen in a purely political context. He did not rule out the industrialists as possible allies. Such an alliance was feasible depending on future developments. He wanted to keep all doors open, but did not intend to step through them blindfolded. To understand how Mussolini kept that option open, we must look briefly to the period between 1914 and 1918.

When Mussolini was expelled from the Socialist party in November 1914 because of his belief that the party ought to abandon its commitment to neutrality and favor intervention in the war, he found himself isolated. Unwilling to renounce his Socialist faith (he justified his interventionism on the ground that war would hasten the outbreak of social revolution in Italy), yet forced by circumstances and temperament to forge his own way in politics. Mussolini drifted from Socialist ideological orthodoxy. The decisive break (although he may not have seen it as such at the time), occurred in the aftermath to the military defeat of Caporetto in October 1917.

---

[22] On the financing of the Fascist movement, see Renzo De Felice, "Primi elementi sul finanziamento del fascismo dalle origini al 1924," *Rivista Storica del Socialismo,* VII (May–August 1964), 243. De Felice's conclusions have been challenged by Ernesto Rossi, "I mecenati della rivoluzione," *L'Astrolabio,* II (October 25, 1964), 18–26.

[23] Umberto Banchelli, *Le memorie di un fascista (1919–1922)* (Florence: La Sassaiola Fiorentina, 1922), p. 152.

From then on, Mussolini thought less in terms of class conflict and more in terms of how to speed up and maximize the creation of wealth. He became a "productivist"; he came to the conclusion that the achievement of military victory and the solution of the nation's chronic economic and social problems required policies designed to expand production rather than revolutionary programs of wealth redistribution.[24]

Stated in this manner, one cannot argue against the proposition. It goes without saying that, without the expansion of production, programs of wealth redistribution will redistribute poverty and not wealth. Mussolini's productivism, however, was political rather than economic. By assigning priority to the continued and uninterrupted expansion of production, he in effect condemned revolutionary breaks that would disrupt production even temporarily. He no longer thought of changing the system of production but, rather, of making the existing system function more efficiently.

Productivism marks Mussolini's transition from his original revolutionary radicalism to his subsequent stand as the man of law and order. As a productivist he claimed that anyone who really wanted to raise the general standard of living could not in good conscience condone radical economic and social experiments that threatened to disrupt production. By accepting productivism, he could move in the direction of capital (the constructive "captain of industry" eventually became one of the heroic figures of Fascist mythology) without turning against labor.

Productivism was a concept ideally designed to transcend the Marxist concept of the class struggle. Fascist leaders developed a disturbing ability to differentiate between the interests of the workers, which they claimed were identical with those of the national community that included capital, and the interests of labor organizations. Fascist leaders Italo Balbo and Dino Grandi, whose squads attacked and destroyed countless labor union headquarters, cooperatives, and community centers throughout the Romagna, al-

---

[24] The political significance of Mussolini's productivism is discussed in Renzo De Felice, *Mussolini il rivoluzionario (1883–1920)* (Turin: Giulio Einaudi, 1965), pp. 392–395, 405–418. The significance of the concept of productivism in the development of Fascist ideology is discussed in A. James Gregor, *The Ideology of Fascism: The Rationale of Totalitarianism* (New York: The Free Press, 1969), pp. 147–149, 161–163, 180.

ways insisted they destroyed them because they were the breeding grounds of a subversive political ideology, not because they were centers of popular power, a distinction that was lost on their victims and that does not alter the historical significance of Fascist violence.

But in 1919 Mussolini was not ready to dwell on the conservative implications of economic productivism. As long as revolution was in the air, he did not wish to remove himself from the revolutionary forces. The Fascist program of June 1919 featured many demands that were much too radical to be acceptable to cautious businessmen. Among other demands, the Fascist program called for the introduction of the eight-hour work day, old age and disability pensions, the participation of workers in the management of the factories, a virtually confiscatory progressive tax on capital, and the abolition of the monarchy.

The radical orientation, and the lack of internal discipline characteristic of the Fascist movement in its early days, explain why so few industrialists were involved in the founding of the various *fasci*. Industrialists were not noticeably present when Mussolini inaugurated his first *fascio* in Milan on March 23, 1919. The Fascists of Genoa did not enjoy the confidence of the powerful Perrone brothers. There was closer rapport in Turin; a number of industrialists were present at the inauguration of that *fascio* on March 29, 1919. According to one Fascist observer in Turin, "the industrialists were the Fascists or, rather, some members of the industrial class were." [25] But this same writer also comments that the industrialists in that city were Fascists only because they approved the movement's antisocialism, not because they really understood the Fascist mentality.

As a description of the attitudes shared by the industrial leadership and fascism, the term antisocialism is vague and misleading. Questions of political doctrine had little to do with the matter. The political convergence of organized industry and fascism was rooted in the day to day realities of Italian life during the postwar period. In the first place, fascism was never the doctrinal antithesis of social-

---

[25] Raoul Ghezzi, *Comunisti, industriali e fascisti a Torino, 1920–1923* (Turin: Ditta Eredi Botta, 1923), p. 5. Also, *Il Popolo d'Italia*, March 24, 1919, pp. 1–2; March 30, 1919, p. 5. The industrialists' hostility to fascism is stressed in Piero Melograni, "Confindustria e fascismo tra il 1919 e il 1925," *Il Nuovo Osservatore*, VI (November–December 1965), 834–873.

ism. Mussolini attacked the Socialist party for its continued polemic against the war, for its internationalism, and for its political tactics at home, but he usually professed sympathy for programs of social reform. There is good reason to believe that both before and after the March on Rome he would have welcomed the cooperation of the moderate, reformist wing of the Socialist party and particularly of the Socialist labor unions in the *Confederazione Generale del Lavoro* (CGL). Nor were the industrialists initially against the idea of collaboration with the Socialist labor leadership. They were certainly determined to prevent or defeat a Socialist revolution, but they also took steps to initiate a dialogue with organized labor. In an atmosphere less receptive to ideological arguments than that of postwar Italy, there might have been room for understanding.

The CGII made its debut on the national scene in April 1919 with a number of concessions calculated to convey an image of paternalistic concern for the welfare of the workers. In his inaugural speech, Ferraris ruled out the possibility of changes based on violence and expropriation, but held out the possibility of improvements in labor-management relations. He probably referred to an experiment that was already underway in some large industrial concerns. Fiat, Pirelli, and the Ilva Steel Works had begun to distribute a modest share of stock to their employees. Gino Olivetti was able to convince some of his reluctant colleagues to agree to the introduction of the eight-hour day in industry. The CGII even petitioned the government to provide basic food items such as bread at popular prices regardless of costs of production.[26]

Unfortunately, not all industrialists were disposed to concede. Opposition from within, and a rapidly deteriorating economic and social situation, forced the CGII to retrace its steps. Popular expectations that the conclusion of peace would usher in an era of unprecedented prosperity were quickly dispelled. Heavy industry experienced a decline in production immediately after the war. Full-fledged economic recession began in 1921. Unemployment was high and inflation drove the cost of living to previously unimaginable heights. There was a widespread feeling among the industrial

---

[26] *Corriere della Sera,* February 9, 1919, p. 5; June 8, 1919, p. 5. Also, Franco Catalano, *Potere economico e fascismo. La crisi del dopoguerra* (Milan: Lerici, 1964), pp. 97–101.

leaders that concessions would only encourage a revolution of rising expectations.

Gino Olivetti responded to pressures from within by asking labor leaders in July 1919 not to insist on the immediate introduction of the eight-hour day. At the same time, a member of the CGII's executive committee warned the government against introducing too many price controls.[27] By this time most businessmen were impatient to see all government controls over production repealed. Many industrialists, including Olivetti, were convinced that profit-sharing devices were extremely dangerous because labor looked upon them as a means of introducing workers' control of production.[28]

Profit sharing, introduced in many capitalist countries for essentially conservative purposes, took on revolutionary implications in the context of Italian politics. In Italy the idea of profit sharing imperceptibly merged with the far more revolutionary concept of workers' control of production. That control was to be achieved through the introduction of workers' factory councils. According to Antonio Gramsci, the leading theoretician of the movement to introduce factory councils, these councils were to educate the workers in the responsibilities of power.[29] That was precisely what the CGII wished to avoid and it issued a formal warning to its members that the councils were a devious device to facilitate the introduction of communism by the backdoor. During a major strike in March 1920, Olivetti stated flatly that "there cannot be two powers in the same factory." [30] During that particular strike the labor unions failed to obtain recognition for the factory councils. From that moment on, both sides looked for the decisive showdown that would settle the issue.

The showdown came in September 1920 when the workers took over the factories and tried to run them without the consent of management. The short-lived occupation of the factories proved to

---

[27] *L'Italia Industriale,* I (July–September 1919), p. 25.

[28] *L'Italia Industriale,* II (April 1920), 29, 43, 77–80.

[29] On the genesis of the factory councils, see John M. Cammett, *Antonio Gramsci and the Origins of Italian Communism* (Stanford: Stanford University Press, 1967), pp. 71–95.

[30] Angelo Tasca, *Nascita e avvento del fascismo* (Florence: La Nuova Italia, 1950), pp. 113, 127.

be a decisive turning point for labor, industry, and fascism. Labor emerged defeated and demoralized; the industrialists felt the shock of temporary expropriation and lost faith in the ability of liberal governments to protect them against revolution; Mussolini, who at first had sympathized with the workers, sensed that the revolutionary tide was turning and that the future belonged to a political movement that posed as a viable alternative to both socialism and liberalism.

The industrialists had their share of responsibility for the occupation of the factories. The dispute had begun in June 1920 with the CGII's refusal to consider a request for a wage increase. Labor retaliated with a slowdown of production (apparently marked by scattered acts of sabotage against machinery), whereupon the industrialists decided to escalate the conflict by calling a lockout. The first lockout occurred at the Romeo automobile plant in Milan on August 30. Giovanni Agnelli, supported by a group of diehards who seemed to welcome an all-out confrontation with labor, decided to extend the lockouts to Turin. At that point, the occupations increased beyond control and the country seemed to be on the verge of revolution.[31]

The threat of revolution was probably more imagined than real. The workers were improvising, their leaders were hesitant, and the Socialist party was divided. The industrial leadership was angry but did not panic. Ettore Conti, who was then the president of the CGII and who masterminded industrial strategy in the negotiations with labor and government officials, was confident of victory. When, at the very height of the crisis, the labor leader Bruno Buozzi facetiously urged Conti to join the revolution, Conti replied that "the Italian bourgeoisie is not like the Russian . . . while there was no real bourgeoisiè in Russia, we, luckily for our country, have one that is cultured, intelligent, hardworking, and determined to prevail." [32]

What shocked and angered the industrialists even more than the seizure of their factories, was Premier Giovanni Giolitti's refusal to use force against the occupiers. There is good reason to believe that

[31] *Il Popolo d'Italia,* September 1, 1920, p. 3; September 2, 1920, p. 1.
[32] Conti, *Dal taccuino di un borghese,* p. 238.

the industrialists welcomed the illegal seizure of the factories as a means of forcing Giolitti to commit the army and the police against the workers and thereby abandon his customary policy of neutrality in labor conflicts.[33] Giolitti's refusal to play the role of *deus ex machina* meant that the industrialists had to negotiate with the workers on the one issue that was absolute anathema, the introduction of the factory councils. The intransigents within the CGII insisted that to negotiate meant conceding that factory councils were feasible at least in principle, and that it was precisely the principle of the undisputed and undivided authority of management they wanted to preserve. Conti, who was equally opposed to the factory councils, was more interested in the substance than in the principle of the matter. He agreed to negotiate, provided both sides were to have equal representation in the negotiating commission. Giolitti agreed. The negotiators were promptly deadlocked and the debate was transferred to parliament where it continued until the March on Rome. After the Fascist takeover, the subject was quietly shelved.

Conti's faith in the Giolittian manner and in the efficacy of temporization was justified in the long run. But not everyone shared Conti's coolness in the face of danger. The lower middle classes feared that the occupation of the factories signalled the beginning rather than the end of large-scale revolutionary action. Propertied interests began to understand the possible consequences of political liberalism. If the open society meant a steady drift toward socialism, then they wanted none of it. What was needed was a strong, authoritarian government capable of resisting the pressure of popular demands. The industrialists did their part to turn the alleged weakness of liberal government into the great political issue of the moment.

Both Nitti and Giolitti, who represented the two main liberal alternatives of the postwar period, were accused of demagogy by the business press. Giolitti in particular came under fire, not only for his failure to support the employers during the occupation of

---

[33] The bad feelings between Giolitti and the industrialists are discussed in Paolo Spriano, *L'occupazione delle fabbriche. Settembre 1920* (Turin: Giulio Einaudi, 1964), pp. 31–33, 39–41, 53–55.

the factories, but also for his fiscal and social policies. Two tax laws sponsored by Giolitti and introduced soon after the occupation of the factories in September 1920 were resented in business circles. The first law provided for the registration of stocks and bonds in the name of the owner and was designed to close a tax loophole beneficial to the well-to-do. The second law introduced virtually confiscatory tax rates on business profits accumulated during the war. This second measure could never be effectively enforced, but its presence on the books created insecurity among employers. It indicated Giolitti's willingness to humor popular resentments against businessmen who had allegedly enriched themselves while the soldiers were risking their lives in the trenches. The second law was denounced by the business press as economically irresponsible demagogy.[34]

When it came to welfare and social security measures, the industrialists argued that it was the duty of every employer to provide for the security and well-being of his workers, the implication being that there was no need for massive public expenditures in this area. Public welfare programs diverted scarce capital resources from productive business investments into economically wasteful social programs; they drained the national treasury and brought the country to the verge of bankruptcy; and (strange argument) Italian workers were too politically immature to shoulder their fair share of the cost of a comprehensive system of social security.[35]

Giolitti was also alarmed by the rising costs of social programs but he was unwilling to curtail them as drastically as the industrialists would have liked. In February 1921 he took the politically courageous step of abolishing extensive government subsidies to farmers introduced after the war to keep down the price of bread. Beyond that he would not go. He was prepared to placate his business critics by extending special tax incentives, lowering transportation rates, and increasing protective tariffs, but he did not reverse his social policies. In his final message to parliament, just before the elections of May 1921, which dealt him the final and most serious setback of his political career, Giolitti reaffirmed his commit-

---

[34] ASIA, *Relazione sull'opera svolta dall'Associazione nell'anno 1920*, pp. 8–13, 17–19.

[35] CGII, *Annuario 1922*, pp. 142–143.

ment to continued public support of workers' cooperatives, land reform, social welfare, and factory councils. But business wanted a government willing to pursue policies that were bound to be unpopular but necessary to achieve what they claimed was a wiser allocation of economic resources.

And that was precisely the kind of government Mussolini began to promise in the second half of 1920. The intransigent hostility of his former Socialist comrades and his intuitive awareness that the revolutionary wave had spent itself have been cited as possible reasons for his decision to steer the Fascist movement in a more conservative direction.[36] Whatever the reasons, Mussolini shed some of his earlier hesitancy to associate openly with businessmen. Mussolini's candidacy in the political elections of May 1921 was sponsored by a Milanese industrialist, Senatore Borletti. Thirty-five Fascists, including Mussolini, were elected to parliament.

Mussolini was most persuasive and a number of leading industrialists became convinced "Mussolinians." Ettore Conti's description of Mussolini, dated January 7, 1922, is revealing.

A man of his disposition, who defends the gains of our military victory, who opposes the agricultural workers' leagues which threaten the physical safety of landowners, and imperil their goods and their crops, who is against the introduction of the regime of the hammer and sickle, who trusts the elites more than the masses, is made to order for the Confederation of Industry. Such, at least, is the opinion of Giovanni Silvestri, my successor to the presidency of the Confederation.[37]

But the confidence the industrialists had in Mussolini personally did not extend to all his followers. Mussolini's authority over the Fascist *ras,* as the local bosses of the movement were called, was tenuous at best. Some were more than happy to look after the interests of the local gentry, but others were headstrong and unpredictable. Even a conservative *ras* like Cesare Maria De Vecchi, who controlled the Fascist organization in Turin and who was a protagonist of the March on Rome, refused to go along with Mussolini's

---

[36] Guido Dorso, *Benito Mussolini alla conquista del potere* (Turin: Giulio Einaudi, 1949), pp. 218–223. Also, Massimo Rocca (pseud. Libero Tancredi), *Come il fascismo divenne una dittatura* (Milan: Edizioni Librarie Italiane, 1952), pp. 77–108.

[37] Conti, *Dal taccuino di un borghese,* pp. 262–263.

plans for winning the confidence of business. He nursed a personal grudge against Giovanni Agnelli and made no effort to hide it. When an industrial representative showed up at Fascist headquarters soon after the occupation of the factories with generous offers of financial aid, De Vecchi had him ejected from the premises with an unceremonious kick in the behind.[38] De Vecchi was a great believer in the therapeutic value of Fascist violence.

The industrialists were equally suspicious of the numerous revolutionary syndicalists who flocked toward fascism, and through whose efforts fascism developed a following among agricultural and industrial workers. The first Fascist labor union was organized in the Romagna in February 1921. Given the questionable accuracy of Fascist figures that claim agricultural and industrial workers represented 39.7 percent of the party membership in November 1921, the fact remains that that year saw the first Fascist popular grass-roots movement. Labor leadership remained hostile to big business.[39]

If fascism could boast any following among workers, credit for it belongs to Edmondo Rossoni, an enigmatic figure in the enigmatic, colorful history of Italian radicalism. Like Mussolini, Rossoni began his political career as a Socialist. But, unlike Mussolini whose interests were primarily political and for whom labor unions were a means to an end, Rossoni was dedicated to the organization of labor. His interest in labor had survived his disillusionment with Marxist doctrine. He had travelled to the United States in 1912 with the intention of organizing Italian workers in American cities. He was then still a firm believer in the Marxist doctrine of the international solidarity of the proletariat but his experience in New York City disillusioned him. He came to the conclusion that Italian workers in America were exploited not only by their capitalist masters but also by fellow workers of other nationalities.[40]

With his faith in the international solidarity of the proletariat shattered, Rossoni turned from Marxism to Sorelism. Sorelian

---

[38] Cesare Maria De Vecchi di Val Cismon, "Mussolini vero," *Tempo,* XXI (November 10, 1959), 44.

[39] Renzo De Felice, *Mussolini il fascista.* I. *La conquista del potere, 1921–1925* (Turin: Giulio Einaudi, 1966), pp. 6–11.

[40] Edmondo Rossoni, *Le idèe della ricostruzione. Discorsi sul sindacalismo fascista* (Florence: Bemporad, 1923), pp. 10, 59.

syndicalists were already active in Italy under the leadership of Filippo Corridoni and Alceste De Ambris. Corridoni died in combat during the First World War and De Ambris eventually turned away from fascism disillusioned with Mussolini's lack of revolutionary enthusiasm. Rossoni stayed on even though he too had doubts about Mussolini. He did not hesitate to pick up followers in the wake of the destructions perpetrated by Balbo's fascist *squadristi* in the Romagna at the expense of Socialist labor unions and cooperatives. At first Rossoni tried to remain autonomous, but in January 1922, he agreed to bring his followers into the Fascist party.[41]

Rossoni's conversion to fascism was probably motivated by his desire to prevent fascism from moving completely to the Right. In order to play an effective role within fascism, Rossoni had to endorse the political formulas developed by Mussolini after his turn to the Right, particularly Mussolini's productivism and its logical corollary of class cooperation. These formulas were broad enough to permit different interpretations. While the industrialists expected the workers to do most of the cooperating, Rossoni and his followers looked at it the other way around. Rossoni hoped to coerce the employers into joining the Fascist corporations, thereby depriving them of their organizational autonomy and bringing them under the control of the Fascist party. Rossoni's prime target was the CGII. For this reason, the industrialists looked upon the Fascist syndicalists as the fly in the ointment.

Given the aims of Fascist syndicalism and the lack of discipline within the party, full-fledged political cooperation between industry and fascism had to be ruled out even after Mussolini had decided to veer in a conservative direction. But there was nothing to prevent an understanding on economic issues to which most Fascist activists were indifferent. This economic understanding matured within the Parliamentary Economic Alliance, the parliamentary rallying ground of the elected representatives of fascism and big business. The Alliance's program, issued in June 1922, featured a long list of demands including lower taxes on business to stimulate

---

[41] Sorel's influence on Italian fascism is discussed in Jack J. Roth, "The Roots of Italian Fascism: Sorel and Sorelismo," *Journal of Modern History,* XXXIX (March 1967), 30–45.

production, transfer of public transportation and communications networks (particularly the profitable urban telephone lines) to private enterprise, drastic reduction of public expenditures, a balanced budget, reform of the state bureaucracy and the judicial system, lower costs of production, and a halt to the issuance of government bonds which drew capital away from the private sector of the economy. The program was perfectly summed up in its request urging "the relinquishing by the state of every function which is not strictly necessary." [42] It was an endorsement by the business and the Fascist leadership of total classical economic liberalism.

The demands of the Alliance, though overtly dealing exclusively with economic issues, if implemented, would have had far-reaching social and political repercussions. Balancing the budget could have been an euphemism for curtailing social security programs, a reform of the state bureaucracy could have meant the elimination of social agencies, expanding production by reducing taxes on business could have meant relying on indirect taxes having a disproportionately high incidence on low-income groups. Such a program of economic reform, if followed to its conclusions, in effect would have reversed established political and social trends.

Fascism and industry were obviously closer than they had ever been before. Yet, neither side saw itself as being dependent upon the other. Each maintained a distinct political profile and tried to play its own political game. The industrialists had full confidence in their ability to weather any future political crisis. During 1922, the CGII's public statements revealed a new self-assurance which occasionally bordered on arrogance. When a general strike called by the anti-Fascist labor unions on July 31, 1922 quickly collapsed after a bad start, the CGII warned that the industrialists were now a political power to be reckoned with. "And it is high time," commented the CGII, because "the industrialists are tired of seeing in-

[42] CGII, *Protocollo 550, Circolare 300*, dated June 28, 1922. From Volume II of a collection of mimeographed circulars to the membership, available for consultation in the library of the CGII in Rome. Also, *O. I.*, January 1, 1922, p. 7; February 1, 1922, p. 2; April 15, 1922, p. 8; October 1, 1922, p. 5. On Fascist support for the program of the Alliance, see *Opera Omnia*, XVIII, 264–265. The composition of the Alliance is described in Ernesto Rossi, *Padroni del vapore e fascismo* (Bari: Laterza, 1966), pp. 39–40.

dustry treated as a *corpus vile* on which every social experiment is permissible." [43]

Even the Fascists were not entirely exempt from the CGII's criticism. The industrialists now claimed for themselves the primacy in the struggle against communism and chastised verbally those political groups (obviously the Fascists) who were said to have entered the fray after the danger of revolution had subsided. The concluding blast in that statement illustrates the optimism prevalent in industrial circles shortly before the March on Rome. It also indicates that the industrialists, rightly or wrongly, saw themselves as an autonomous political force:

Political parties must begin to understand that it will not be possible for them to thrive at the expense of industry. If they have not learned from past experience, we may have to carry out another rescue operation, and this time we will know who is on our side.

THE STAGING OF THE MARCH ON ROME

During the month preceding the March on Rome the industrialists intensified their attacks against the government. Organized labor was no longer their primary concern, nor did they still fear the possibility of revolution. The government had replaced organized labor and socialism as industry's *bête noire*. On September 25, 1922 the CGII renewed its criticism of government monopolies and singled out that on life insurance as being particularly unjustified (probably because it was a highly profitable operation). The CGII also urged the government to overhaul the administration of the railroads but did not demand their transfer to private enterprise (no doubt because of the railroads' enormous deficit). [44]

These and other requests were publicized by means of a national industrial convention held in Milan on October 17. Reform of the public administration was the central theme to which the various speakers addressed themselves at the CGII's request. The CGII had specified that "Unless this problem is solved by radical measures,

---

[43] *O. I.*, August 15, 1922, p. 1.
[44] *O. I.*, October 1, 1922, p. 5.

we cannot hope for the stability of public finance, the economic reconstruction of the country, and the efficient resumption of production." [45]

The speakers followed the cue. There was a great deal of talk about the need to restore a sense of discipline and hierarchy to all levels of government, an insistence which betrays the authoritarian mentality with which the industrialists approached the problem of government. In their dissatisfaction with liberal government, few of them stopped to reflect that the line between authoritarianism and totalitarianism is a thin one.

The sense of urgency and the tone of confidence evident in these appeals suggest that the industrialists had decided that the time had come to drive home the attack against the politicians in Rome at the same time that the Fascists were preparing to stage their March on Rome. But there is no evidence that Fascists and industrialists had in any way coordinated their movements. There were influential industrialists who still had reservations about the Fascist movement. A comparison of the program of the Liberal party in which such leading industrialists as Benni, Donegani, Mazzini, and Olivetti were active, with the Fascist party's program of October 21, 1922 shows how similar the economic viewpoints of business and fascism were on the eve of the March on Rome. The liberal program stressed the "greatness of the country" idea, the need to strengthen the authority of the state, and the importance of balancing the budget. But it also stated that private initiative should be regulated in the national interest in order to enable private enterprise to revitalize the national economy.[46]

The ambiguity of this last point is apparent. The Liberal party, the traditional exponent of economic laissez-faire, apparently made a concession to the advocates of public regulation of private enterprise, with the typical Fascist twist that this regulation must aim at making private enterprise more efficient. Not everyone within the Liberal party was willing to go that far. A difference of opinion on this score had emerged during a preparatory conference. Rumors that the Fascists were preparing a *coup d'état* were already in the

---

[45] CGII, *Protocollo 604, Circolare 309,* II, circular dated October 8, 1922. Also, *Il Secolo,* October 18, 1922, p. 4.

[46] *La Stampa,* October 22, 1922, p. 1.

air and pro-Fascist liberals wanted their party to side openly with the Fascists in the impending crisis. Mazzini disagreed. He pointed out that fascism included the most diverse elements and that until its internal contrasts had been clarified no one could foretell in which direction fascism might ultimately move. He posed the troubling question, "How can we, men of the Right, say without hesitations that fascism is a party of the Right and not, perhaps, really a political party of the Left?" [47]

Mazzini's question summed up the dilemma facing the industrial leadership as the Fascists moved to take advantage of the political crisis precipitated in part by the industrialists' lack of confidence in the government. Doubts about the real nature of fascism troubled the industrialists to such an extent that they even tried to bring Giolitti back into power. The prefect of Milan, Alfredo Lusignoli, who was known to enjoy Giolitti's confidence, was approached around October 10 by a delegation of industrialists which included Benni, Conti, Olivetti, Pirelli, and Targetti. They told Lusignoli that fascism should be "channelled" at once, which presumably meant that Fascists should be invited to participate in government. They thought that Giolitti should head the new government in order to forestall a major political crisis with unpredictable consequences. They also stated that the necessities of the moment required "the action of strong men and not compromises . . . for the sake of idle parliamentary maneuvers. They fear, in one word, the return of men who . . . are discredited by their own precedents." [48]

The appeal to Giolitti was indicative of the industrialists' political confusion. Was not Giolitti himself one of those men "discredited by their own precedents?" Was it possible for Giolitti to form an energetic government at a time when the balance of forces in parliament tended to produce a virtual paralysis of the political system? Giolitti could form a stable government only by engineering a coalition of his own followers, catholic Popularists, and Socialists. Such a solution was precluded by, among other things, the industrialists' stipulation that Fascist representatives be brought

---

[47] *La Stampa,* October 11, 1922, p. 1.

[48] Message from Lusignoli to Giolitti, reproduced in Nino Valeri, *Da Giolitti a Mussolini. Momenti della crisi del liberalismo* (Florence: Parenti, 1958), p. 164.

into the government. No Socialists, and probably not many Popularists, would have agreed to participate in such a government. It might have been possible for Giolitti to go either to the Right or to the Left, but not in both directions at once. By asking for an energetic and authoritarian government, the industrialists were in effect asking for the kind of government that could be formed only by disregarding parliament and by illegal means. Although they probably did not realize it, only Mussolini could give them what they wanted.[49]

Mussolini prepared the ground before making his move. In a calculated effort to reduce the opposition and to minimize the risks in case of failure, he went out of his way to reassure outside groups that they had nothing to lose, and perhaps much to gain, from a Fascist take over of the government. Rossoni and the Fascist syndicalists were the biggest obstacle to an understanding with the industrialists. However, Rossoni was sufficiently cooperative. In July 1922, the Fascist syndicate for seamen signed a new labor contract with Genoese shipowners whereby the seamen lost overtime compensation for work performed in conjunction with docking operations. In August, the CGII expressed the hope that Italian workers might find wiser leadership in the Fascist syndicates than they had found under socialism.[50]

On September 25, the CGII adopted a resolution condemning any attempt to monopolize the representation of labor.[51] In this case, the CGII championed freedom of association for the workers and argued that every worker had the right to join the labor union of his choice. In principle, the CGII's statement was a challenge to Socialist and Fascist labor organizers because both groups wanted to monopolize the representation of labor. In practice, Fascist labor organizers stood to gain because they had made little headway among industrial workers. With the support of the employers, the

---

[49] Paolo Alatri, *Le origini del fascismo* (Rome: Editori Riuniti, 1956), pp. 170–172. The industrialists' commitment to Giolitti during the March on Rome is stressed in De Felice, *Mussolini il fascista*, I, 327–331, and Melograni, "Confindustria e fascismo," p. 842.

[50] *O. I.*, February 15, 1922, p. 1; March 1, 1922, pp. 6–7; August 15, 1922, p. 1; September 1–15, 1922, p. 9.

[51] *O. I.*, October 1, 1922, p. 5.

Fascists were now in a position to move in wherever the Socialist unions disintegrated.

In spite of their mutual suspicion, industrialists and Fascist syndicalists began to understand the advantages of cooperation. Rossoni declared himself a convinced productivist and stressed the importance of rewarding individual achievement in the factory. The industrialists inferred from this that Fascist labor leaders would be less demanding than their Socialist rivals when it came to collective, across-the-board gains. The industrialists had much to gain from the application of Fascist elitism to labor relations. In mid-October Rossoni asked the CGII to cooperate in a joint effort to increase the productivity of the workers by improving their technical training. It was a modest proposal and reassured the industrialists about the reasonableness of Fascist labor leaders. Rossoni and Olivetti met at least once before the March on Rome in conjunction with Rossoni's proposal.[52] It was the beginning of a tense coexistence between two hostile forces determined to mould fascism each in its own image.

Mussolini was eager to extend his personal assurances that business had much to gain from a Fascist victory. On October 26, just as the Fascist columns were beginning to march on Rome, Mussolini spoke to a group of industrialists headed by Benni and Pirelli. The conversation turned to the prosaic topics of the level of currency exchanges, the quotations of government bonds, and the nation's credit abroad. According to Pirelli's subsequent reconstruction of the interview, the industrialists "were filled with admiration upon discovering a man who could discuss these problems with profound understanding and with a keen awareness of their complexity and importance." [53] According to the only other account of what transpired at this meeting, Mussolini assured the industrialists "that the aim of the impending Fascist move was to reestablish discipline particularly within the factories and that no outlandish experiments . . . would be carried out." [54]

---

[52] *Il Secolo,* October 19, 1922, p. 6. For a perceptive discussion of how Fascist elitism applied to labor relations, see Ubaldo Formentini, *Gerarchie sindacali* (Turin: Gobetti, 1923).

[53] *O. I.,* November 30, 1932, pp. 703–704, and *Riv. Pol. Econ.,* XXII (November 1932), 1171–1178.

[54] Cesare Rossi, *Mussolini com'era* (Rome: Ruffolo, 1947), p. 120. Also by the

The fact that the interview took place after the Fascists had decided to march on Rome precludes the possibility of a previous political understanding between Fascists and industrialists. Had there been such an understanding, there would have been no need for Mussolini to extend reassurances at the very last moment. But the fact that the industrialists went to be reassured also suggests that they had no fundamental objections of principle to a Fascist take over. They may not have been Fascists at heart, but neither were they plain, old-fashioned liberals as many of them claimed after the fall of the regime.

Mussolini's shrewd tactics assured him the acquiescence of the industrial leaders in his bid for power. They did not encourage Mussolini to make his decisive move, but once he had made it, they were prepared to consider him as just another candidate for the job of prime minister, a candidate who could obtain their tacit support in return for specific economic concessions. It was simply a business transaction to be settled with minimum fuss. In other words, the industrialists transposed the habits of commercial intercourse to politics and, in so doing, displayed an astonishing lack of political sensitivity. With their eyes fixed on the economic contingencies of the moment, they disregarded the vital political principles at stake. In a sense, they were duped by Mussolini the crafty politician. It makes as much sense to say Mussolini made use of the industrialists as it does to say the industrialists manipulated Mussolini. Each had something that the other wanted. While to the industrialists economics was everything, to Mussolini everything was politics.

During the most critical days of the March on Rome (October 27-29), Benni, Conti, Olivetti, Pirelli, and other prominent industrialists played a valuable supporting role at Mussolini's side in Milan. King Victor Emmanuel, Prime Minister Luigi Facta, and Antonio Salandra who was being considered for the premiership, all received messages from the industrialists in Milan expressing support for Mussolini. But when we look closely at the sequence of events, there can be little doubt that throughout those confusing days Mussolini remained at all times the prime mover on the Fas-

---

same author, see the article in the daily *Il Tirreno* (Leghorn), November 18, 1955, pp. 1, 8.

cists' side. So long as the possibility existed that the government might declare a state of siege and suppress the insurrection by force, the industrialists let themselves be guided by the maxim that discretion is the better part of valor. They expressed support for Mussolini, but cautiously and by means of secret personal messages.

When on Saturday morning, October 28, rumors began to circulate that the state of siege had been proclaimed, the industrialists, "somewhat alarmed by the turn that events were taking," went to confer with Mussolini. But when they reached his office they learned that the rumors were false and that Mussolini had decided to settle for nothing less than the prime ministry; (until then no one had discarded the possibility of solving the crisis by turning over just a few ministries to the Fascists). Only later, in the afternoon of that day, the CGII and the General Confederation of Italian Agriculture issued a bulletin publicly supporting the Fascists. By that time, although the king was still toying with the idea of offering the premiership to Salandra, his refusal to employ force had already given the game to Mussolini.[55]

On October 31, the CGII issued an enthusiastic endorsement of the new government and, above all, of the new leader:

It [the government] springs from the youthful energies of the nation and is dominated by the Will of their Leader. *It is to him that we must look hopefully* at a time when the economic and financial problems of the nation are more urgent and vexing than ever before.[56]

A most striking and generally unnoticed feature of this proclamation is that the word "fascism" never appears in it. It looks as if the industrialists wanted to keep that troublesome element out of the picture. The CGII's statement praised the new government's commitment to "the right to own property, the general obligation to work, the need for discipline, the advancement of private initiative, loyalty to the nation"—it endorsed the authoritarian and nationalistic commitments shared by both groups and the economic principles implicit in the last-minute political deal between Mussolini

[55] This reconstruction of the events is based on information from *Corriere della Sera,* October 30, 1922, p. 1; November 2, 1922, p. 2. Alfredo Rocco, *Scritti e discorsi politici* (Milan: Giuffrè, 1938), II, 745–746. Antonio Salandra, *Memorie politiche, 1916–1925* (Milan: Garzanti, 1951), pp. 24–25.

[56] *O. I.,* November 1, 1922, p. 1 (emphasis added).

and the industrialists. Mussolini's concessions to big business could not go unchallenged within fascism. Fascist syndicalists, intellectuals, and dissatisfied *ras* began to speak soon after the March on Rome of the "second wave" of the Fascist revolution. According to the advocates of the "second wave," the March on Rome was only a beginning; the real revolution would in fact wipe away all those tactical concessions to vested interest groups which were motivated by political expediency.

The industrialists preferred to look upon the March on Rome as the closing act or, even better, as the curtain call of the Fascist revolution. They hoped it would mark the end of social unrest and weak government, and signal the return to normalcy. Mussolini impressed them as being a practical politician who was not likely to risk the antagonism of the country's economic leadership merely to pursue some political abstraction. In this respect, his often demonstrated political flexibility and pragmatism were his most reassuring traits. He seemed best equipped to keep his radical followers under control—hence, the CGII's desire to bolster his authority and prestige is evident in its proclamation of October 31. In years to come, the industrialists would turn to Mussolini with a fervor that can only be described as religious. But there was little mysticism in their outlook. Through Mussolini they hoped to exert leverage on the entire party.

Giovanni Agnelli is reported to have said, "We industrialists are government supporters by definition." [57] On the basis of this maxim of practical wisdom, the CGII was bound to cultivate good relations with the Fascist political leadership after the March on Rome. It was now more necessary than ever to persevere in the dialogue with fascism in order to keep it on the path of economic orthodoxy. The CGII intended to play the role of watchdog and, to play it effectively, it had to extend and tighten its representational control over industry. If it could claim to speak for all industry, it could then penetrate into the institutional fabric of the Fascist state from a position of greater power with little fear of losing its independence. The economic and social reality of Fascist Italy emerged in large measure from the continuing tension between the CGII and fascism.

---

[57] Guarneri, *Battaglie economiche,* I, 57.

II

FORGING A RELATIONSHIP:
YEARS OF TENSION AND ADJUSTMENT
(1922–1926)

Mussolini's behavior after the March on Rome continued to be assuring. In his speeches before the Chamber and the Senate he promised precisely that mixture of energetic authoritarianism and respect for constitutional formulas which the industrialists had been demanding since the end of the war. When speaking to the elected Chamber, where the Socialist opposition was still strong, he was domineering and arrogant. In front of the traditionally conservative Senate (senators were all appointed by the king), he was firm but deferential. He carefully cultivated the image of a politician aware of limit and measure.[1] Italians who had been dismayed by the alleged weakness of previous governments were delighted. Curbing the excesses of parliamentary freedom without curtailing it altogether was just the right salve for consciences troubled by the Fascists' disregard for constitutional niceties displayed during the March on Rome. In view of Mussolini's restraint, the CGII retro-

---

[1] Mussolini's initial speeches in parliament as prime minister appear in *Opera Omnia,* XIX, 17–25.

actively welcomed the event as a long overdue national catharsis, and celebrated it by introducing a new system for numbering its circulars, a gesture which suggested a desire to wipe the slate clean and begin anew.

The success of the March on Rome aroused great expectations among industrialists. They flocked to Rome, eager to establish personal contacts with Fascist political personalities. Some cautious businessmen urged their more aggressive colleagues to exercise restraint and return to their factories where their services were needed.[2] By its very nature the CGII was far more interested in promoting collective rather than individual gains. The new government was certainly receptive to its immediate demands. Three days after Mussolini's appointment as premier, the new Council of Ministers unanimously revoked Giolitti's law requiring the registration of stocks and bonds in the name of the owner. On November 10 the government announced that the telephone lines would soon be turned over to private enterprise. On November 14 Mussolini decided to end the parliamentary investigation on the accumulation of illegal war profits. The data collected by the investigators was impounded by the government and has never been released. That same day, the government also announced that it would soon abolish public regulation over the operations of life insurance companies. Subsequently, the government relinquished its monopoly over the production and sale of matches, discontinued price and rent controls, lowered inheritance taxes, and suspended the land reform.[3]

A dose of adrenalin had suddenly been injected into the Italian political system. Measures which had been debated or stalled in committees for years were enacted almost overnight. Industry was perhaps the major beneficiary of this spectacular outburst of government activity. The full significance of these economic concessions cannot be appreciated without relating them to the broad reformist aspirations shared by fascism and the business leadership. It would be misleading to think of the industrialists as a reactionary group. They accepted fascism not only because it had helped to restore law and order, but also because it promised to cut through many

---

2 *La Finanza Italiana,* XVI (October 25, 1924), 399.

3 Guarneri, *Battaglie economiche,* I, 87–88.

ideological Gordian knots and rapidly reform the apparatus of government. Ideological debate tended to question the validity of the existing system of economic, political, and social relations, while administrative reform aimed at making that same system efficient and operational. Fascist reforms before 1925 aimed at correcting or eliminating flaws which prevented the system from functioning smoothly.

The reformist aspirations of fascism were expressed in a number of ways. Whenever Mussolini presented himself to the public behind the wheel of a racing car, or piloting an airplane (only bad weather prevented him from flying to Rome when the king invited him to form a government during the March on Rome), or driving a tractor, as he was fond of doing, he was saying in effect that the nation had at last found a leader capable of coping with the complexities of a technological society. Mussolini's theatrical gestures actually expressed technocratic aspirations which were always latent, although never dominant, in Italian fascism. These technocratic aspirations were summed up in the slogan *largo alle competenze* (make way for competence) which was popular in Fascist circles during the early years of the regime.[4]

The man who bravely struggled to translate these aspirations into tangible guidelines was Alberto De Stefani, Mussolini's minister of finance from October 1922 to July 1925. De Stefani's program was coherent. It was inspired by a laissez-faire philosophy which, in principle, was totally acceptable to business. Public enterprise was to give way to private initiative wherever possible. Public controls over production were to be abolished. Restrictions in the scope of governmental action would make it possible for the government to reduce and reform the bureaucracy, thereby gaining greater administrative efficiency and lowering operating costs. The reduction of public expenditures was to be accompanied by fiscal reform, which was to increase government revenue by the paradoxical device of actually lowering tax rates and simplifying tax laws. De Stefani's rationale was that unrealistically high tax rates and complicated tax laws reduced revenue by encouraging widespread

---

[4] The technocratic current in fascism is discussed in Alberto Aquarone, "Aspirazioni tecnocratiche del primo fascismo," *Nord e Sud,* XI (April 1964), 109–128.

cheating and by making it virtually impossible for government officials to verify tax returns. The objective was to balance the budget,
a feat that would end the threat of inflation and restore economic
and social stability. He promised a *politica della lesina* (a policy of
tight spending), and the CGII urged him to apply it relentlessly "in
all fields and toward all classes." [5]

De Stefani was by no means subservient to the industrialists. He
was a former professor of economics and a Fascist *squadrista* with
a reputation for personal independence. He was not well known in
business circles and did not feel at home among businessmen. His
personal relations with the Perrone brothers and with Pirelli were
strained. Furthermore, De Stefani took economic laissez-faire seriously, more seriously than many businessmen who were always
ready to pay lip service to the doctrine but who were more interested in securing high protective tariffs, concluding agreements in
restraint of trade, and obtaining government contracts.

Although from the industrialists' point of view De Stefani may
not have been the ideal person to occupy the Ministry of Finance,
there was little in his policies they could object to at first. Tight
spending would presumably curb inflation, thereby lowering the
cost of imported raw materials and semifinished products. It would
also help channel badly needed investment capital from the
public to the private sector of the economy. De Stefani precisely
harped upon this last point when he told a gathering of bankers
that a balanced budget would enable the government to cut down
on the emission of paper currency and government bonds. A greater
share of private savings would then flow into industrial investments. [6] The enthusiasm and support aroused in business circles by
De Stefani's austerity program were evident from Conti's optimistic
view of the future:

Savings will now return to production. . . . A [balanced budget] will
strengthen our credit abroad, facilitate the purchase of raw materials
needed by our industries, and channel capital toward productive investments. By facilitating the reduction of our public debt, [a balanced
budget] raises the possibility that we might be able to reduce the ab-

---

[5] *La Stampa,* November 9, 1922, p. 1.

[6] *Il Sole,* May 19–20, 1924, p. 3.

normally high interest payments which now burden our treasury, and may thereby enable the Ministry of Finance to lower tax rates.[7]

Businessmen were not the only group that welcomed the prospect of administrative and fiscal reform. Parliament also was willing to grant Mussolini the power to rule by decree in order to simplify and rationalize the public administration. Mussolini promised quick action. There is no reason to doubt Mussolini's intention to live up to his mandate. Unfortunately, good intentions cannot compensate for the lack of ideas. On the Fascist side, De Stefani was the only leader with a plan and with the administrative ability to implement it. The rest, including Mussolini, were torn between their desire to eliminate the imperfections of the existing system and their urge to live up to their image as revolutionists and proceed to a radical restructuring of the state. The result was confusion and rivalry between the warring factions of the Fascist party.

Under these circumstances, it was inevitable that Fascist efforts at reform should suffer from the interference of outside pressure groups pursuing well-defined objectives. The industrialists were by no means the only pressure group determined to "tame" and manipulate the Fascists (the monarchy, the Church, the army, the public administration, and even parliament had their particular axe to grind). But the industrialists were singularly well equipped to deal with the Fascists—they were well organized and well led, and had an *entrée* into Fascist circles. These were important tactical advantages and they were brought to bear, first of all, on De Stefani's administrative reforms.

THE POLITICS OF ADMINISTRATIVE REFORM

Bureaucratization seems to be an unavoidable by-product of our collective pursuit of material well-being. Unfortunately, the restrictions which bureaucracy imposes on personal freedom often conflict with the individualism that is part of our cultural heritage. The conflict between bureaucracy and individualism has been a constant theme in the history of modern Italy. The conflict was,

---

[7] *Il Sole,* May 22, 1924, p. 3; June 5, 1924, p. 1

and still is, felt strongly throughout Italian society. The fact that Mussolini seized upon this issue to extract from parliament a mandate for his government to rule by decree shows that he understood its universal appeal and timeliness. Businessmen simply wanted the government to remove resented economic controls, but public opinion also sympathized in an ambivalent way with any attempt to deal with the vexing problem of bureaucratic regimentation. Fascism, with its puzzling combination of retrogressive and progressive tendencies, voiced the ambivalence of a general attitude aware of both the inescapable necessity and the irritating consequences of bureaucratization. Fascism articulated this ambivalence by promising to restrict and at the same time to revitalize the domain of bureaucracy.

Although in the long run fascism actually doubled the size of the bureaucracy and compounded the problem of bureaucratic inefficiency, immediately after the March on Rome Mussolini's government subjected the public administration to a searching reappraisal. As in so many other instances, fascism played the role of executor rather than initiator. The reform guidelines applied under Mussolini had been outlined by parliamentary committees as early as 1921. Parliamentary investigators had urged the government to simplify administrative procedures and to concentrate power in the hands of fewer ministries. The CGII had gone on record as favoring this type of reform as early as 1919.[8]

But in politics decisions are rarely made on merit alone. How the central administration actually was reorganized reveals that, though rationalization and simplification were the stated objectives, political motivations and partisan interests were also at work. The industrialists took a particular interest in the operations of transportation and communications facilities. The Fascist government set up a new agency, the Ministry of Communications, which had jurisdiction over the postal services, telegraphs, telephones, railroads, and the merchant marine. This ministry became the industrialists' special preserve. From May 1924 to May 1934 it was

---

[8] *L'Italia Industriale,* I (July–September 1919), 6. The best discussion of these initial reforms appears in Alberto Aquarone, *L'organizzazione dello Stato totalitario* (Turin: Giulio Einaudi, 1965), pp. 5–11.

run by Admiral Costanzo Ciano (the father of Galeazzo Ciano who became Mussolini's minister of foreign affairs in the late 1930's). Costanzo Ciano, a World War I naval hero, equally at home in industrial and Fascist circles, worked out the details of the transfer of the profitable telephone lines from the state to private enterprise. The state retained only the unprofitable long-distance lines. From January 1935 to November 1939 the post was held by Benni who began the large-scale electrification of the railroads.

The most revealing feature of the administrative reform was the abolition, in April 1923, of the Ministry of Labor and Welfare. The ministry had been the target of attacks from the business press since the time of its founding in June 1920. The CGII welcomed its demise on the grounds that it had been too costly, served no useful purpose, and had been established for purely political reasons to appease subversive elements.[9] Labor and welfare fell under the jurisdiction, first, of the Ministry of Industry and Commerce which was a traditional stronghold of business, and subsequently, of the Ministry of the National Economy established in August 1923. The new ministry replaced three formerly separate ones by uniting under the same roof agriculture, commerce, industry, labor and welfare. Labor thus lost its autonomous seat of power in the public administration. The pursuit of administrative efficiency had facilitated the attainment of a long-standing political goal of the industrial leadership.

In addition to favoring a concentration of power in fewer hands, the industrialists also wanted this power to be placed in the right hands. The appearance of the new Ministry of the National Economy was not greeted enthusiastically by all industrialists. Many of them objected to concentrating so much power in the hands of a single minister. The unprecedented concentration of power made it important for the industrialists to have the right man in that position. Mussolini reassured them by appointing a man in whom the industrialists had complete confidence, the liberal economist Mario Orso Corbino. Benni remembered with pleasure how during the occupation of the factories of September 1920 Corbino had

---

[9] CGII, *Annuario 1924* (Rome: Cooperativa Tipografica Egeria, 1924), pp. 283–285.

been an uncompromising opponent of negotiations with labor on the ground that to agree to negotiate on the issue of factory councils amounted to a betrayal of the sacrosanct principle of private ownership.[10]

The CGII took great interest in the staffing of secondary agencies in the public administration. In November 1922, the industrialists won strong representation in the Superior Council of Labor and Welfare which served as an advisory body to the Ministry of Labor and Welfare. The position of labor representatives was weakened further after labor and welfare were transferred to the Ministry of the National Economy. Of the forty-five appointments to the Superior Council of the National Economy, a full two-thirds went to business, with labor receiving no more than nine seats.[11] As if that were not enough, the representatives of labor were confined to the ministry's section for labor and welfare. The ministry's remaining sections (industry, agriculture and forestry, commerce, credit and insurance), were staffed almost exclusively by representatives of the business groups which would be directly affected by the ministry's policies, a clear example of regulation by the regulated. Labor was excluded from these sections on the questionable ground that its absence would facilitate the frank discussion of economic problems. The CGII expressed its satisfaction with the government's decision to accept virtually all its nominees to this important body.[12]

The reform of the central administration was not without repercussions at the local level. There, an effort was made to redefine and expand the power of provincial and municipal administrations. The most interesting local reform dealt with the status and functions of the chambers of commerce. The chambers of commerce were purely private associations of businessmen which usually represented industrial and commercial interests. A government decree of May 8, 1924 transformed them into agencies of the Ministry of the National Economy and changed their name to Provincial Councils of the Economy. They became public agencies endowed with

---

[10] *Il Sole,* April 14–15, 1924, p. 2.

[11] *O. I.,* December 1, 1922, p. 1; February 1, 1924, p. 2. *Il Sole,* February 1, 1924, p. 1; May 9, 1924, p. 3.

[12] CGII, *Annuario 1924,* pp. 285–286.

advisory functions to be exercised for the benefit and at the request of the Ministry of the National Economy.[13]

Many industrialists viewed the abolition of the chambers of commerce as a threat to the principle of private initiative. They wondered whether this was not the beginning of a Fascist drive to gain control of organized business. Their fears were compounded by their knowledge of Fascist plans to introduce labor representatives into the Provincial Councils. That reminded the industrialists of Rossoni's plans to establish the corporative state, an eventuality which they were not yet prepared to accept.

In the reform of the chambers of commerce the CGII could not remain indifferent. Avoiding once again a frontal attack that would have involved the industrialists in embarrassing confrontations with the Fascists, Benni and Olivetti went to work in parliament to modify and delay the project. With the support of other conservative elements, they were able to keep the reform within acceptable limits. Their delaying tactics prevented passage of the bill until April 1926. By that time, the reform of the chambers of commerce was a secondary feature of a larger plan to restructure the Fascist state. In that larger context, the industrialists actually gained from the reform of the chambers of commerce. Corbino had already pointed out to them that the real purpose of the reform was to strengthen the influence of business on government. That is precisely what happened. Workers' representatives were not admitted to the reformed chambers of commerce until June 1931, and then only to their own separate section that could deal only with questions of labor. Labor had no advisory role as far as economic questions were concerned. The industrialists even managed to squeeze out spokesmen for commercial interests.[14]

The Provincial Councils, as marginal to the business of government as they may have been, were still the first institutional links between the public and private sectors. In theory, their existence

---

[13] Aquarone, *L'organizzazione dello Stato totalitario,* p. 139.

[14] *Il Sole,* May 7, 1924, p. 1. Olivetti's position can be construed from his speeches in the Chamber. See *Atti. Camera,* 1924–1926, V, 4805–4814. Giuseppe Belluzzo, who was the minister of the national economy when the parliamentary debate took place, argued that the industrialists gained control of many chambers of commerce as a result of the reform, *Ibid.,* 4795. Commercial interests complained that the industrialists were too powerful in the reformed

was incompatible with the principle of entrepreneurial autonomy. In practice, they were an additional channel through which businessmen could influence the government. By controlling the Provincial Councils, the industrialists controlled the local eyes and ears of the central administration. As an example of how the industrialists turned a potentially dangerous measure to their own advantage and of how labor was relegated to a subordinate position in agencies that were theoretically designed to represent a broad cross section of society, the Provincial Councils are the corporative state in microcosm. From their vantage points in the public administration, the industrialists were now in a stronger position to influence the government.

INDUSTRY AND FASCIST ECONOMIC POLICY, 1922–1925

It is imperative that we determine the relative power of the business an dthe Fascist leadership as precisely as possible. To argue that the industrialists widened their access to the centers of administrative power is not to suggest that they had become the undisputed policy-makers. On the contrary, they had opposition from many quarters. The Ministry of Finance often pursued its independent course. Labor, commerce, agriculture, and even small industry often opposed the economic policies favored by the CGII.

De Stefani's great merit, as far as the industrialists were concerned, was that he spoke the language of economic development rather than social reform. At a time when the economic advantages of deficit spending were not generally recognized, De Stefani's policy of tight spending, coupled with his avowed productivism and economic liberalism, seemed the best route to the expansion of production. Not only did De Stefani's course conform to prevailing economic thought, it was a logical and inescapable consequence of Mussolini's political tactics. Mussolini was too shrewd a politician to risk political isolation by failing to live up to the promises made to Fascist supporters and sympathizers in business circles. Hence,

---

chambers. See Confederazione Generale del Commercio Italiano, *Atti del Congresso Nazionale di Roma del 21–22–23 maggio 1925* (Rome: Tipografia della Camera dei Deputati, 1925), pp. 90–91. Guarneri, in *Battaglie economiche*, I, 141–143, as usual overlooks the industrialists' practical gains and stresses instead the anti-laissez-faire implications of the reform.

the unmistakable probusiness bias of De Stefani's fiscal policies, a bias which, according to Mussolini, had saved industry 1,260,000,-000 lire in taxes by 1928.[15]

De Stefani believed that a sound fiscal policy must aim at encouraging the accumulation of capital and at favoring investments. Given the fact that the Fascist take over had not been accompanied by any change in the economic structure of the country, this was indeed the only way in which fascism could promote the expansion of production. The absence of an economic dimension to the Fascist revolution meant Fascist acceptance of traditional economics. Within two years of the March on Rome, De Stefani had abolished taxes on the interest paid to foreign investors (social revolutions usually are marked by a rejection of all financial obligations to foreign interests), replaced taxes on luxury products with a general sales tax ranging from two to three percent (sales taxes always fall proportionately more heavily on low income than on high income groups), reduced inheritance taxes, stamp taxes, taxes on the personal incomes of business managers and corporation officials, and had lowered the tax burden of high income groups in general. He had also tackled the difficult problem of municipal taxation. In that area, he abolished the anachronistic tolls levied by local governments on goods transported across municipal lines, a reform that was hailed as a great achievement even by enemies of the regime.[16]

The keystone of De Stefani's fiscal reforms was a new progressive personal income tax *(imposta complementare progressiva sul reddito)* which went into effect on January 1, 1925. The new income tax replaced an older one dating back to 1918. Although the two taxes bore the same name, their characteristics were different. The biggest difference was that the new tax applied only to physical persons; business firms of all descriptions were exempt from it. The exemption reflected De Stefani's productivist thinking. He hoped

[15] *Riv. Pol. Econ.,* XVIII (June 1928), 562.

[16] Needless to say, the industrialists were demanding these fiscal measures. See ASIA, *Relazione sull'opera svolta dall'Associazione nell'anno 1922 in materia di legislazione e consulenza commerciale e tributaria* (Rome: Cooperativa Tipografica Egeria, 1923), pp. 18–20. Also, CGII, *Annuario 1923,* pp. 137–143, and Francesco De Gaetano, "La legislazione tributaria italiana durante l'anno 1922," *Riv. Pol. Econ.,* XIII (January 1923), 72–77. On the municipal tolls, see *Il Sole,* February 1, 1924, p. 1; May 4, 1924, p. 1.

that exempting business firms from the new tax would stimulate production and that the resulting rise in production would be reflected in higher incomes. The government could then tax these higher incomes without interfering with business operations.[17]

De Stefani reasoned that it was fairer and more economically advantageous to tax personal income than business capital. Unfortunately, even as a progressive income tax, De Stefani's new tax betrayed a classist bias. Not only did it fall on all wage earners who benefited only indirectly and unevenly from the government's productivist policies, but it reduced the tax rates for high income groups set by the progressive income tax of 1918. The older law had specified rates ranging from eight to sixteen percent for combined annual personal incomes above 10,000 lire, while the new tax rates varied from a minimum of one percent to a maximum of ten percent for incomes in the same category.

In spite of his obvious desire to facilitate the expansion of production by reducing the tax load on business, De Stefani could not honor all requests reaching his ministry from countless business groups and individuals. The CGII tried to coordinate the flow of requests from industry by filtering them through its office for legal counselling and legislative studies which was set up for that purpose in January 1924. Even so, De Stefani often had to turn down requests for action. He could not accept the CGII's insistent request that his revenue officials abandon "inductive criteria" in their efforts to assess the taxable assets of business corporations, a question which to this day has never been settled to the satisfaction of Italian businessmen.

Revenue investigators suspected that the documentary evidence submitted by business firms in the form of budgets or bookkeeping records was not a reliable indication of their real financial status. Therefore, tax officials preferred to base their estimates on such supplementary "inductive criteria" as money spent by individual businessmen on personal entertainment and luxury products, their general style of living, the size of a firm's labor force, and other highly subjective evidence. The system led to abuses of all sorts and generated bureaucratic corruption but no one knew how to work

---

[17] CGII, *Circolare 356–9*, III, dated March 30, 1925. Also, *Il Sole*, May 22, 1924, p. 3.

out a better one. The CGII, which repeatedly and indignantly denounced its evils, was also reluctant to allow government officials to look closely into the operations of business firms. CGII officials argued that real costs of production must remain secret from one's business competitors and that this secrecy was the essence of private enterprise.[18]

As minister of finance, De Stefani had to take into account the requests of all sectors of the economy, and many conflicted with what the industrialists wanted. He also had to keep in mind the government's financial needs, which meant there was a limit to the number of tax reductions and exemptions he could grant. Consequently, he had to delay or refuse action on a number of specific requests from the CGII. The denied measures included the repeal of a fifteen percent tax on the dividends from unregistered securities, the exemption from taxation of the reserve capital of business corporations, and the extension of special tax allowances on depreciated securities.[19]

Complaints were not slow in coming. The industrialists began by criticizing De Stefani's alleged slowness in moving ahead with a comprehensive program of fiscal reform. Olivetti found De Stefani's progressive income tax inadequate. As early as May 1923, Conti hinted that the pace of reform could be stepped up and that the initiative could come only "from the wisdom and willpower of the Man who has taken on the difficult and noble task of rejuvenating the national economy." [20] Conti's words, by invoking Mussolini's personal intervention, contained an indirect criticism of De Stefani. From then on, there was a crescendo of veiled protests, culminating during the first half of 1925 in public criticism of De Stefani's fiscal, commercial, and monetary policies.

As minister of finance, De Stefani had to keep an eye on the country's balance of payments which was chronically unfavorable. The unfavorable balance of trade jeopardized his efforts to balance the budget and uphold the exchange rate of the lira. The balance of trade could be improved by reducing imports and increasing ex-

---

[18] The debate over the use of "inductive criteria" dragged on inconclusively for years. See *Atti. Senato*, 1929–1933, V, 586–591.

[19] *Il Sole,* January 5, 1924, p. 1; May 9, 1924, p. 3; May 11, 1924, p. 1; May 22, 1924, p. 3; December 8–9, 1924, pp. 3–4. Also, *O. I.*, January 1, 1924, p. 6.

[20] ASIA, *Relazione sull'opera svolta dall'Associazione nell'anno 1922*, p. 34.

ports. In practice, however, due perhaps in part to his well-known free-trade bias, De Stefani seemed more interested in expanding exports than in keeping foreign goods off the domestic market. In March 1923, he abolished duties on refined sugar, a step which turned the politically influential beet growers and sugar refiners into his mortal enemies. Even though he subsequently reinstated these duties in part, the initial repeal betrayed an outlook that was bound to cause concern in industrial circles.

The CGII continued to support the protectionist interests in industry. When in March 1923 the tariff of 1921 came up for discussion in parliament, Benni and Olivetti tried to strengthen its protectionist features.[21] Of course, as Benni never tired of pointing out, few Italian manufacturers could afford to be doctrinaire protectionists. The scarcity of essential natural resources and the uneven development of the various sectors of industry forced Italian manufacturers to rely heavily on imported raw materials, fuels, semifinished products, and machinery. Even steel producers, shipbuilders, and manufacturers of industrial machinery, three of the most normally protectionist groups in the country, had to petition the government to eliminate duties on pig and scrap iron and ball bearings.[22]

Consequently, Benni and Olivetti were not too unhappy when the opposition of free traders, exporting textile interests, agricultural producers, and government officials forced them to drop their request for a radical restructuring of the tariff of 1921. They were happy to settle for important modifications of the existing tariff. Acting on Benni's request, the Council of Ministers authorized the

---

[21] Benni and Olivetti proposed to substitute the most favored nation approach of the tariff system of 1921 with a more protectionist device known as the autonomous tariff. The most favored nation clause meant that the lowest duties extended to any single trading partner would be automatically extended to all other. The autonomous tariff would have established fixed maximum and minimum duties. The minimum duties would have been extended to any nation with whom a commercial treaty was in effect but the duties themselves would not have been subject to negotiation. See *Atti. Camera,* 1921–1923, X, 9041–9042, 9123–9133, 9150–9157, 9250, 9313–9315. The free-trade point of view was expressed by Luigi Einaudi, *Cronache economiche e politiche di un trentennio (1893–1925)* (Turin: Giulio Einaudi, 1965), VII, 139–142, 147–158, 171–177, 228–232, 255–257, 289–294, 308–310.

[22] *Il Popolo d'Italia,* December 31, 1922, p. 4. *La Finanza Italiana,* XV (May 5, 1923), 172; XV (May 12, 1923), 184.

government to adjust duties on particular items without having to consult parliament. That was the kind of *ad hoc* protectionism favored by the CGII. It was an effective way of securing the maximum protection possible with minimum restrictions on the flow of needed materials from abroad; and all this could be done through administrative channels, without undue publicity.[23]

Since across-the-board protectionism was impractical, CGII officials had to bargain hard in order to obtain the most advantageous conditions from the country's trading partners. The Fascist government was quick to start bilateral trade negotiations. The problem was that, in order to secure outlets for textile and agricultural exports, the government often had to open the domestic market to foreign manufacturers. Concessions were bound to be most extensive in the case of highly industrialized trading partners that were also good customers for Italian agricultural exports. Germany was a case in point. Italian manufacturers lived in perpetual fear that Italy might become a dumping ground for German manufactured products. Alberto Pirelli had helped to formulate the famous Dawes Plan of 1924 which specified the actual payments Germany had to make in war reparations. The CGII welcomed the plan precisely because it removed the possibility that the Germans might dump undetermined quantities of manufactured goods on the Italian market.[24]

Benni and Conti, who were at that time presidents of the CGII and ASIA respectively, did their best to explain away the inherent conflict between the exporting and protectionist interests. Benni deplored agriculture's opposition to raising duties on German products and argued that Italian industry was still the best customer of Italian agriculture. In the Senate, Conti dwelled upon the general usefulness of economic protectionism and even quoted from the Old Testament to make his point. His senate colleagues were delighted with this original departure from Dante quotations which were quite frequent in that learned body, but opponents were not

---

[23] *Riv. Pol. Econ.*, XIV (January 1924), 66–68.

[24] ASIA, *Sedici anni di attività fra le Società Italiane per Azioni* (Rome: Cooperativa Tipografica Castaldi, 1929), pp. 109–118. Pirelli, in his book *Dopoguerra 1919–1932. Note ed esperienze* (Milan: Arti Grafiche Ghezzi, 1961), pp. 45–47, mentions only the objections of the British coal producers to German coal shipments to Italy.

convinced.[25] The treaty with Germany had to be signed and Felice
Guarneri, who represented the CGII in the negotiating commission, concluded sadly that Italian industrialists must resign themselves to the unpleasant necessities of economic life.[26]

Unpleasant political necessities also had to be taken into account
by the industrialists. In spite of strong opposition from the CGII,
the government found it politically expedient to conclude economically questionable trade agreements with Austria (April 28,
1923) and Czechoslovakia (March 1, 1924). Mussolini did not hide
his political interest in the Danubian region of Europe where he
hoped to supplant French influence. It should be pointed out that
Mussolini's interest in Eastern Europe did not represent a new
departure in Italian foreign policy. He pursued a long-standing
goal of national diplomacy. The least risky way of pursuing this
goal was to conclude trade agreements that would be economically
advantageous for the countries of the area. In the case of Austria
and Czeckoslovakia, the industrialists objected for essentially the
same reasons that they had opposed the treaty with Germany: the
Italian market would become an outlet for their manufactured products while they would be able to absorb only limited quantities of
Italian industrial products.[27]

The fact that the Italian government concluded these commercial
agreements shows the limitations of the CGII's influence over political decisions. Indeed, the industrialists themselves usually ac-
knowledged the priority of political over purely economic considerations. In the case of his Danubian policy, however, Mussolini
could hold out prospects of economic expansion that might ultimately compensate the industrialists for their losses. With the exception of industrialized countries like Austria and Czeckoslovakia,
Eastern Europe seemed to be a promising market for Italian industrial exports and investment capital. In line with these optimistic
expectations, the CGII set up, in July 1923, an agency for foreign
commerce which immediately received Mussolini's blessings. Con-

---

[25] Benni gave his arguments in his pamphlet, *La politica doganale italiana*
(Milan: Lanzani, 1925), pp. 13–15. Conti's speech appears in *Atti. Senato,* 1924–
1925, III, 2998–3003.

[26] See Guarneri's pamphlet, *La politica degli scambi con l'estero* (Rome: Publisher not given, 1931), p. 17.

[27] CGII, *Annuario 1924,* pp. 182–185.

sular and diplomatic officials were instructed to start gathering economic data on the countries where they resided and to transmit this information directly to the CGII. Government officials also cooperated with the CGII to set up Italian chambers of commerce in the major commercial centers of Eastern Europe.[28] When the government decided to extend a loan to Poland, Benni abandoned his customary reticence and waxed eloquent: "Waving under those skies, [the Italian flag] seems to say to us: Italians, turn to your work! The eagles of Roman civilization now leave the museums and resume their flight across the world." [29]

Apparently, the eagles were expected to fly as far as the Soviet Union. In February 1924, the Italian government extended diplomatic recognition to the Soviet Union and, immediately thereafter, the two countries signed a commercial treaty. Benni was elated at the conclusion of the treaty and argued that, in spite of the modest volume of trade which it envisaged, it might enable Italian manufacturers to establish a bridgehead in a potentially vast market.[30] He was not in the least alarmed at the prospect of entering into a closer relationship with a Communist country. In fact, he hailed the extension of diplomatic recognition to the Soviet Union as evidence of the realism and reasonableness of Fascist foreign policy. Whenever the choice was between ideology and profits, actual or anticipated, Italian industrialists always were willing to sacrifice ideology.

It is difficult to say whether the anticipated profits materialized. Certainly, the economic penetration of Eastern Europe had no noticeable repercussions on the Italian political or social scene in the 1920's. The fact that in that decade Eastern Europe began to absorb increasing quantities of Italian industrial and agricultural products was bound to affect Italian foreign policy in the long run. Perhaps the steps taken in the 1920's to strengthen the Italian economic presence abroad can be seen as a timid precedent or precondition for the more aggressive foreign policy of the 1930's. Economic expansion abroad also suggested itself as a possible solution of the domestic conflicts between business and labor and between

---

[28] *Ibid.*, pp. 197–198. Also, *Il Sole*, April 6, 1924, p. 1; April 10, 1924, p. 3.

[29] *Il Sole*, April 5, 1924, p. 2.

[30] *Atti. Camera*, 1924–1925, IV, 4170–4171. CGII, *Annuario 1924*, pp. 139–140, 185. *Il Sole*, May 4, 1924, p. 1.

rival interests in the different sectors of production. This became a refrain of Fascist political propaganda in the 1930's, with the significant difference that in the 1930's the regime would stress political as well as economic expansion.

For the time being, however, domestic problems were still dealt with by purely domestic means. The industrialists became increasingly dissatisfied with De Stefani's performance as minister of finance. His downfall came partly as a result of his efforts in February and March 1925 to curb a flurry of speculation on the stock market. The resulting market crisis helped to crystallize smouldering resentments against him. In June 1925, De Stefani's hostility to economic protectionism and his fiscal policies were criticized by a number of influential senators.[31] The political situation had changed. Fascism was moving into its totalitarian phase and Mussolini probably felt that a convinced economic liberal like De Stefani would not serve him well. De Stefani's resignation, engineered and announced by Mussolini on July 8, 1925, was part of a general change of the guard. It looked as if the "second wave" of the Fascist revolution was about to reach shore and the industrial leadership prepared to meet it.

INDUSTRY AND FASCIST SYNDICALISM, 1922–1924

The industrialists may have overestimated the potency of the revolutionary charge within fascism. Unlike many opponents of the regime who claimed that Fascist labor organizations were little more than company unions, the industrialists did not dismiss Fascist syndicalism as a paper tiger. Rossoni's behavior after the March on Rome was not reassuring. In his eagerness to move ahead with the social revolution which had not occurred with the March on Rome, he began to enroll both workers and employers in the same syndical associations.

Rossoni planned to carry on his revolution by setting up mixed syndicates of workers and employers (hence, the term "integral

---

[31] *Atti. Senato,* 1924–1925, III, 3110–3124. The business reaction to De Stefani's stock market decrees can be followed in *Il Sole,* March 1, 1925, p. 1; March 2–3, 1925, pp. 1, 3; March 6, 1925, p. 1; March 9–10, 1925, p. 1; March 16–17, 1925, p. 1; July 11, 1925, p. 1. See, also, Publio Mengarini, "Effetti dei provvedimenti sulle borse," *Riv. Pol. Econ.,* XV (June 1925), 517–524.

syndicalism" often used to describe Rossoni's initial objective). The terminology of Fascist social doctrine was never very clear and a few words of explanation are needed. The terms syndicalism, mixed syndicalism, integral syndicalism, and corporativism were used interchangeably in the early 1920's. They all referred to a system that would resolve conflicts between particular and general interests. Through the reforms which fascism was expected to enact, capital and labor would be educated and, if necessary, coerced to think in terms of national rather than class interests.

The confusion of terms evident in the official title of Rossoni's organization which was called the General Confederation of Fascist Syndical Corporations, reflected a serious confusion of ideas. The terms syndicalism and corporativism were differentiated only as a result of unforeseen and largely fortuitous developments. The industrialists, many of whom looked upon this confusion of ideas with a mixture of amusement and concern, had a lot to do with how these terms were eventually defined.

Rossoni exemplified the ambiguities of fascism. In the absence of serious studies on Rossoni, it is difficult to evaluate his contribution to the development of Italian fascism. There is good reason to think, however, that he had simply not thought out the problem of social revolution and that he was willing to borrow ideas here and there to fit the needs of the moment. The concept of corporativism had been developed in Italy by Sorelian syndicalists and by catholic and nationalist theoreticians. When the Nationalist party merged with fascism in 1923, nationalist theoreticians like Alfredo Rocco, Luigi Federzoni, and Filippo Carli continued to elaborate their ideas and tried to steer the Fascist party in their direction. They tried to institutionalize their concept of class cooperation.

Rossoni borrowed their terminology but it is doubtful that he shared their values. Born and bred to the class struggle, he used the corporativist concept of class cooperation as a means to an end. His objective was to destroy the organizational autonomy of big business, thereby eliminating its basis of political power. To him class cooperation meant that big business would have to do most of the cooperating. Furthermore, while the nationalists thought in terms of gradual change by legal means, the syndicalists leaned toward revolutionary violence. There was a definite contrast between these two components of fascism and the industrialists exploited it to their advantage.

Whatever his shortcomings as an ideologist may have been, Rossoni was an able tactician and the industrialists feared him for it. In his day-to-day behavior, Rossoni tried not to repeat some of the serious errors committed by the Socialists. Although his rhetoric was often denunciatory and rabble-rousing, he did not engage in agitation for its own sake. Nor did he fall victim to a doctrinaire hostility toward the middle classes, particularly white collar workers, technicians, and small businessmen. He tried to bridge the gap between these middle class groups and the agricultural and industrial proletariat, an experiment which has been tried with some success in Italy since the Second World War. Speaking at a Fascist rally in Bologna in November 1922, Rossoni referred to the middle class as the "brains of the nation" and urged them to join his syndicates.[32] Had they done so, big business would have been left isolated and vulnerable.

Rossoni's partly successful efforts to enroll an undetermined but probably sizable number of employers from agriculture, commerce, and small industry into his mixed syndicates convinced CGII officials that they should take steps to protect themselves. They had their own plans with regard to small industry and did not want Rossoni to infringe on their exclusive preserve. The CGII issued instructions to all industrial associations to avoid direct contacts with Fascist authorities and to clear their political commitments and contributions with CGII headquarters.[33] At the same time, the CGII stepped up its recruiting program in small and medium industry. Pressure tactics were used where blandishments failed. Printers and manufacturers of silk textiles agreed to join only after the CGII threatened to boycott their trade associations.[34]

But the decisive battle against Rossoni was fought and won by Benni in the political backstairs of the regime. Mussolini was in-

---

[32] *Il Popolo d'Italia,* November 12, 1922, p. 3.

[33] CGII, *Circolare 328,* II, dated May 25, 1923; *Circolare 330,* II, dated May 25, 1923; *Circolare 351,* II, dated September 10, 1923. On Rossoni's mixed syndicates, see Abrate, *La lotta sindacale nella industrializzazione in Italia,* pp. 379–381, and League of Nations. International Labor Office, *Freedom of Association* ("Studies and Reports." Series A, No. 31; Geneva, 1928), IV, 29–30.

[34] CGII, *Circolare 754,* II, dated October 11, 1923; *Circolare 755,* II, dated October 11, 1923. Also, *Il Sole,* May 9, 1924, pp. 3, 4.

itially in favor of mixed syndicates but, as he had little intrinsic interest in labor problems, he could be swayed by political considerations. Sometime in March 1923, Benni approached Mussolini and reminded him that the industrialists had supported him only because fascism had accepted private enterprise which could not be reconciled with Rossoni's mixed syndicates. Mussolini, not yet sufficiently entrenched in power to feel he could dispense with the industrialists' support, quickly changed his mind. He reassured Benni that the CGII "is not to be touched or diminished" and that Rossoni would continue to cooperate with the industrialists.[35]

From then on Rossoni had to fight a defensive battle. On November 15, 1923, the Fascist Grand Council came out in favor of preserving the organizational autonomy and integrity of the CGII. On December 19, 1923, the CGII and Rossoni's Confederation of Syndical Corporations signed a pact—the agreement of Chigi Palace—whereby the two organizations promised to "increase their efforts to organize the industrialists and the workers, respectively, for the sake of mutual cooperation." [36] In other words, workers and employers were to be organized separately. The realization of the corporative state receded into the dim and distant future. Rossoni's integral syndicalism had received its fatal blow.

Rossoni did not readily resign himself to defeat. He lashed out at the industrialists whom he accused of being crypto-Marxists: "They find it more convenient to leave the employers on one side and the workers on the other. . . . Marx said the same thing; if the bourgeoisie accepts the separation of the classes, it must not complain about the existence of the class struggle." [37] Meanwhile, his lieutenants in the provinces continued to act as if they still expected the employers to join the Fascist syndicates. Fascist labor leaders from Turin accused the Industrial Federation of Piedmont and the CGII of being enemies of fascism because of their unrelenting opposition to integral syndicalism.[38]

Rossoni could only obtain compensation for his losses. The Fas-

---

[35] *O. I.*, April 1, 1923, p. 5. Mussolini's wavering support of Rossoni's plans is documented in *Opera Omnia*, XIX, 171–175, 212–213.

[36] The text of the agreement appears in *Ibid.*, XX, 132–135. The text of the Grand Council resolution of November 15, 1923 appears on p. 96 of the same volume.

[37] Rossoni, *Le idèe della ricostruzione*, p. 33.

[38] Abrate, *La lotta sindacale nella industrializzazione in Italia*, pp. 384–386.

cist Grand Council demanded in its already mentioned resolution of November 15 that the industrialists grant preferential treatment to the Fascist syndicates. Rossoni, who had personally sponsored the Grand Council resolution, hoped to entice workers away from their Socialist and Catholic labor unions with the help of the employers. Although the industrialists granted Rossoni's request in part, neither they nor their workers were eager to give Rossoni a monopoly of representation.[39] The industrial workers in particular displayed a remarkable loyalty to their Socialist organizations.

Industrialists and Fascist syndicalists thus formed an ambiguous relationship wherein they were both antagonists and collaborators depending on the observer's point of view. An insider noticed the contrasts, an outsider the affinities. Neither could gain mastery over the other. The industrialists were strong enough to protect their organizational independence, but not so invulnerable that they could afford to ignore all of Rossoni's demands. The syndicalists could not force the CGII to surrender, but they had enough leverage to obtain valuable concessions.

In the final analysis, neither side could dispense with the other. From the industrialists' point of view, the presence of the Fascist syndicates helped to keep the labor movement divided. For this reason, most of them were not averse to favoring the expansion of Fascist syndicalism. The problem was how to do so without jeopardizing their freedom of action and without strengthening Rossoni to the point that he might be able to dominate the developing dialogue. In order to keep that dialogue going, CGII officials never dismissed Fascist proposals out of hand. Shortly after the March on Rome, Fascist labor leaders and moderate Socialists tried to fuse Rossoni's Confederation of Fascist Syndical Corporations with the CGL. The fusion was sponsored by the poet and national hero Gabriele d'Annunzio who, ensconced in his luxurious villa overlooking Lake Garda, revelled in the role of spiritual father of Italian fascism. Mussolini was not irrevocably opposed to the union of the two organizations. Olivetti commented that a strengthening of organized labor implied a strengthening of organized industry. In

---

[39] Years later Benni stated that the main purpose of the Chigi agreement had been to favor the expansion of Fascist syndicalism at the expense of the Socialist labor movement. See *Atti. Camera,* 1929–1931, IV, 4532.

other words, the union was possible, provided the industrialists received *quid pro quo*.[40]

That the industrialists' initial suspicion of Fascist syndicalism was waning is evident from the fact that Benni and Olivetti, on July 26, 1923, suggested to the Fascist Grand Council that the CGII and Rossoni's Confederation of Fascist Syndical Corporations should establish "permanent contacts." [41] The advantages of working closely with the Fascist syndicalists were many. Unlike the Socialists who raised all sorts of thorny questions of principle and who demanded far-reaching concessions, the Fascist labor leaders were usually willing to settle for modest wage increases. Rossoni's outbursts and pretensions could not hide the fact that strikes declined rapidly in number during 1923. Consequently, it is not surprising that many industrial associations preferred to deal with the Fascist syndicates.[42] The CGII announced on November 28, 1922 that it would honor all current labor contracts but that it would not negotiate new ones when these expired. When new ones were negotiated, the Fascist syndicates were often recognized as the sole bargaining agents for the workers.[43]

The industrialists needed the government's support to gain representational control of those industrial groups that were still outside the CGII. After signing the Chigi Palace agreement, Rossoni conceded that integral syndicalism was no longer on the Fascist agenda. Olivetti chimed in with the clincher that "the industrialists will be organized by the CGII; ambiguities and misunderstandings on this score are now dispelled." [44] Immediately afterward, the CGII warned the owners of printing establishments that unless they joined they would be denied the CGII's protection and their labor contracts would not be considered valid.[45] In January 1924, the government stopped an attempt to set up an independent association of small and medium industry which, had it developed, would

---

[40] *Opera Omnia*, XVIII, 363–364. *Il Popolo d'Italia*, December 6, 1922, p. 1; December 8, 1922, p. 1. *La Stampa*, December 8, 1922, p. 1.

[41] *Opera Omnia*, XIX, 336.

[42] CGII, *Annuario 1924*, pp. 300–302; *Annuario 1925* (Rome: Cooperativa Tipografica Castaldi, 1925), pp. 174, 515–543.

[43] *Il Popolo d'Italia*, November 29, 1922, p. 4. *Il Sole*, April 10, 1924, p. 3.

[44] *O. I.*, January 1, 1924, p. 2.

[45] *Ibid.*, p. 6.

have been an annoying rival to the CGII. Benni commented in a letter to the CGII's members that the government's intervention "ends any attempts to set up rival organizations and to organize the industrialists either within commercial or mixed associations." [46] That was the last challenge of the CGII's monopoly in the Fascist era.

The available evidence indicates that we should question a recent tendency of Italian scholars to emphasize the dissatisfaction of the industrial leadership after the March on Rome (the works by Mario Abrate, Renzo De Felice, and Piero Melograni are good examples of that tendency). Granted the industrialists were dissatisfied with the performance of the Fascist syndicalists, some extremist *ras,* and even De Stefani, the fact remains that the industrialists' gains, in the form of a business oriented fiscal policy, a pragmatic labor leadership, an authoritarian government willing to support the CGII's membership drive, and a *Duce* who was understanding and occasionally deferential toward the industrial leadership, unquestionably outweighed the losses. Between the March on Rome and the outbreak of the Matteotti crisis in the summer of 1924, the industrialists and the Fascists prepared the groundwork for a closer understanding that reached completion after the Matteotti crisis was settled.

A look at what happened shortly before and after the national elections of April 6, 1924 reveals the closeness of that working relationship. Mussolini, who wanted the industrialists completely on his side, assured Benni that he would personally see to it that nothing threatened the CGII.[47] The industrialists reciprocated by increasing their financial contributions to the Fascist party. One small industrialist complained that all industrial firms connected with the CGII were required to support the Fascist campaign by contributing a fixed percentage of their receipts. Rumor had it the ASIA alone turned over twenty-five million lire to the Fascist party.[48]

---

[46] Letter dated January 23, 1924, found among the CGII's numbered circulars, Volume II.

[47] *Il Sole,* February 27, 1924, p. 1.

[48] *La Giustizia* (Socialist daily of Reggio Emilia), August 29, 1924, p. 2. The ASIA figure is mentioned in Luigi Sturzo, *Italy and Fascismo* (London: Faber and Gwyer, 1926), p. 171.

Benni, Mazzini, Olivetti, and numerous other industrialists entered the elections on the national list sponsored by the Fascist party. Mazzini, who shortly before the March on Rome had expressed strong reservations about fascism, now went over completely. He argued that the industrialists should not persevere "in that agnosticism that has harmed us continuously for twenty years. It is our duty to support a government dedicated to the realization of a Greater Italy. Then we will be entitled to that position within it which is rightfully ours." [49]

The national list composed of Fascist candidates and their allies from other political parties obtained 4,600,000 votes, equivalent to approximately 65 percent of the votes cast. The elections were marred by Fascist violence and intimidation, but marked the first time that fascism won a clearcut victory at the polls. With fascism securely in power, the industrialists took another significant step. The CGII and the Confederation of Fascist Syndical Corporations agreed on May 15, 1924 to recognize each other "as the representatives of industry and organized labor respectively, for the purpose of promoting economic discipline and national greatness." [50] The term "exclusive representation" was avoided because neither side was prepared to grant the other a bargaining monopoly, but the trend in that direction was unmistakable.

The day after the conclusion of the new agreement, Benni spoke out with exceptional firmness against those industrialists who still refused to join the CGII: "We know that some industrialists remain outside our organization precisely because they wish to preserve what they euphemistically call their freedom of action. Let us be on guard lest their lack of discipline harm not only themselves but . . . all of industry." [51]

Now the road seemed clear. The electoral victory removed the

---

[49] *O. I.,* February 15, 1924, p. 6. When some industrialists complained that their group was not adequately represented on the electoral list, Mussolini assured them that the absence or presence of some names was no indication of his government's attitude toward industry. See *O. I.,* March 1, 1924, p. 5. *Il Sole,* February 27, 1924, p. 1. *La Stampa,* February 6, 1924, p. 3. Benni must have been satisfied with Mussolini's assurances because he mobilized the full organizational resources of the CGII to insure a smashing electoral victory for the Fascists. See CGII, *Circolare 886,* II, dated April 3, 1924.

[50] *O. I.,* June 1, 1924, pp. 4–5.

[51] *Ibid.,* p. 1.

aura of illegality that had surrounded fascism. The industrialists, as most people in Italy, probably expected that fascism would shed its revolutionary overtones and proceed gradually and cautiously with reform. Gradual reform carried out with due regard for their interests and demands did not frighten the industrialists. Their experience with fascism in power indicated that they had sufficient political clout to take care of themselves. Under the circumstances, a close working relationship with fascism entailed few risks and many advantages.

Within a matter of days, the political situation changed dramatically.

THE MATTEOTTI MURDER AND THE CRISIS OF FASCISM

As anyone familiar with the history of Fascist Italy knows, the assassination of the Socialist leader Giacomo Matteotti by a gang of Fascist thugs on June 10, 1924 precipitated a major political crisis. As it became clear that leading Fascist personalities including Mussolini were implicated either directly or indirectly, a wave of moral revulsion spread across the country. The political vacuum that developed around Mussolini nearly brought down his government. Individual industrialists like Ettore Conti, Giacinto Motta, and Gian Giacomo Ponti, all from the electrical industry, were among the first to waver in their support of fascism. Even so, they refused to support the Aventinian secessionists (mostly Socialists) who abandoned parliament in protest. As a group, the industrialists did not seem to be particularly alarmed. Their collective silence earned them an indignant rebuke from Luigi Einaudi, a liberal opponent of fascism, who accused them of complicity with Fascist violence. A few industrialists then spoke up publicly, some for and some (all minor figures) against fascism. Some expressions of regret appeared here and there in little-read industrial journals. Giovanni Silvestri, a former president of the CGII, replied that the industrialists had better things to do than to concern themselves with politics and that, in any case, fascism provided the kind of strong government that an undisciplined people like the Italians needed.[52]

---

[52] Einaudi, *Cronache economiche e politiche di un trentennio*, VII, 765–769, 784–789. For other comments by industrial personalities, see *Ibid.*, 780–783, *La Giustizia*, August 29, 1924, p. 2, and *La Tribuna*, August 29, 1924, p. 2.

Silvestri's tactless reply was a blunder. Olivetti was the first to realize that the industrialists could not remain indifferent to politics at such a crucial moment. Mussolini also resented the industrialists' silence. He expected them to give him their full support. What looked like moral complicity to the moralist Einaudi, was proof of disloyalty to Mussolini. When a delegation of Fascist labor organizers from Turin approached him on July 19, 1924 and complained that the industrialists of their city were uncooperative, he accused the industrialists in general of ingratitude toward his regime which had done so much for them. He concluded with the ambiguously ominous words: "If the industrialists reject class cooperation we will have to search for other means. It takes two to collaborate." [53]

The meaning of Mussolini's words quickly became clear. Prompted by Rossoni who sensed an opportunity to even the score with the industrialists, Fascist labor leaders began to instigate strikes throughout northern Italy. The second half of 1924 witnessed a return of labor unrest (from 200 strikes in 1923 to 355 in 1924).[54] Olivetti answered Mussolini's charges with customary adroitness. He began by denying that the industrialists had any hostile intentions toward fascism, and concluded with the remark that under the circumstances the Fascist syndicates could not be accepted as the sole bargaining agents for labor. He explained that the Fascist syndicates would receive special consideration only to the extent that they would demonstrate by their actions that they were truly motivated by the spirit of class cooperation.[55] Strictly speaking, he did not go back on any previous commitments because the industrialists had not yet recognized the Fascists as the sole bargaining agents for labor. But in view of the established trend in that direction, he turned the clock back to the days following the March on Rome when industrialists and Fascist syndicalists had engaged in open power struggle.

The CGII took no public stand during the Matteotti crisis but Gino Olivetti prevailed upon his hesitant colleagues to take a most unusual step in secret. He drew up a secret memorandum which,

---

[53] *La Tribuna*, July 20, 1924, p. 6.

[54] League of Nations. International Labor Office, *Conciliation and Arbitration in Industrial Disputes* ("Studies and Reports." Series A, No. 34; Geneva, 1933), p. 447.

[55] *La Tribuna*, July 23, 1924, p. 1, and *O. I.*, August 1, 1924, p. 1.

together with Benni, Conti, and Pirelli, he brought and read to Mussolini on September 9, 1924. When stripped of its rhetoric, the memorandum was a plea for the restoration of law and order, the continuity of existing political institutions, the suppression within fascism of all revolutionary aspirations and disorderly factions, and for freedom of association particularly among the workers.[56]

The tone and content of the memorandum make it clear that the industrialists were not motivated by a question of political principle but by a fear that a continuation of the crisis would lead to social disorder and the disruption of production. Their concern rested not only on the already mentioned upsurge of labor unrest, but on the fact that during the summer of 1924 the stock market experienced a panic and prices and wages began to rise. Fearful of taking steps that might precipitate disorders throughout the country, they neither supported the opposition on the Aventine nor asked the king to dismiss Mussolini. Their only open move was a purely personal one by Ettore Conti who concluded a senate speech on December 3, 1924 by demanding Mussolini's withdrawal: "Your work of reconstruction will not be preserved by prolonging your stay in power but, rather, by your having created those conditions which assure the country real tranquillity under justice and peace." [57]

With the exception of Conti, the industrialists could not bring themselves to ask for Mussolini's resignation. Their reluctance stemmed from their fear that the fall of fascism might mean the resurgence of socialism. With their fear of revolution, they could see only the alternative between fascism and socialism. Rather than risk a Socialist comeback, they preferred to keep Mussolini and rely ultimately "on true Fascist normalization." [58] Their remonstrances were meant to be interpreted by Mussolini as an indication that he ought to stop wavering and conclude the crisis with a de-

---

[56] The existence of the memorandum had been questioned until recently when Dr. Mario Abrate found a typewritten copy in the archives of the Industrial League of Turin. For the full text of the memorandum, see Abrate, *La lotta sindacale nella industrializzazione in Italia,* pp. 485–488. See, also, De Felice, *Mussolini il fascista,* I, 676–678, 691n, and Melograni, "Confindustria e fascismo tra il 1919 e il 1925," pp. 855–859.

[57] *Atti. Senato,* 1924, I, 346–348. Also, Conti, *Dal taccuino di un borghese,* pp. 321–332.

[58] De Felice, *Mussolini il fascista,* I, 640.

cisive gesture. He continued to hesitate until his own lieutenants warned him that unless he took the initiative to silence the opposition they would take it without him. Then, in his well-known speech of January 3, 1925, he assumed personal responsibility for the misbehavior of his followers and promised the speedy enactment of a new political order. The "totalitarian phase" of fascism was about to begin.

THE EMERGENCE OF THE SYNDICAL STATE, 1925–1926

Major constitutional changes occurred after January 1925. As far as the relationship between organized industry, labor, and government is concerned, the changes marked a continuation rather than a radical departure from what had evolved before the Matteotti crisis. Far from being fully absorbed into the Fascist state as the idea of totalitarianism implies, organized industry managed to retain a degree of autonomy. If the Fascist state turned out to be considerably less totalitarian in practice than it was in theory, the reasons are to be found in Mussolini's political techniques and in the resistance and resourcefulness displayed by outside groups, foremost among them the industrialists.

Mussolini approached the question of institutional change more as compromiser and arbitrator than as committed reformer. He acted more as the manager of a corporate enterprise than as a political leader pursuing well-defined objectives. By January 1925, he understood the need for change because most of his followers were determined to have it so and because there was no other way of solving the political crisis. The *ras,* the leaders of the Fascist militia, syndicalists, intellectual revisionists like Giuseppe Bottai, and nationalists like Alfredo Rocco and Luigi Federzoni, all wanted change, although they were by no means agreed on the nature of the change. Mussolini responded to these demands in September 1924. He appointed a special Commission of Fifteen, later replaced by a Commission of Eighteen (nicknamed Commission of Solons), to study possible constitutional reforms. Aware that Fascist labor organizers were particularly dissatisfied over the lack of support from the top (two of them, Tullio Cianetti and Arnaldo Fioretti, who would soon play important roles in the Fascist labor movement, even considered the possibility of merging with the CGL in the summer of 1924), Mussolini began to take more of an interest in social problems and addressed several workers' rallies.[59]

On January 23, 1925, the Fascist Grand Council issued a statement deploring the fact that some employers were allegedly sabotaging the work of the Fascist syndicates and commented that these problems will be solved permanently by major institutional changes.[60] Such statements annoyed and alarmed the industrialists. There is no evidence that they objected to the demise of the liberal state on philosophical or moral grounds, but they were afraid of reforms carried out by elements hostile to private enterprise and implemented without the advice and consent of the business leadership. The reforms before the Matteotti crisis had been introduced with the consent of the industrialists; after January 1925 there seemed to be a danger that the new reforms might be carried out against them. Olivetti had gone on record in December 1924 as being in favor of politically unaffiliated labor organizations, a view which could not please the Fascists at a time when they thought of allowing only Fascist associations to operate freely. The CGII review *Rivista di Politica Economica* featured articles criticizing Fascist plans to introduce compulsory membership of workers and employers in government-sponsored associations.[61]

The Fascist answer to the industrialists' criticism was a series of strikes that were practically authorized by Mussolini and by the Grand Council. The most spectacular was the steel strike of March 1925 which was joined by the Socialist Industrial Federation of Metal Workers. For a few days, it looked as if the unity of the labor front had been restored. The Fascists eventually pulled out of the strike after having obtained a modest wage increase because by that time the strike had served its political purpose. The industrialists were reminded that socialism was still a force to be reckoned with among industrial workers. A few weeks after the strike, Benni remarked how the industrialists had recently heard voices which

---

[59] *Ibid.*, I, 666–670. Also, *Opera Omnia*, XXI, 56–59, 102–105, 124–125.

[60] *Ibid.*, XXI, 250–251.

[61] Giovanni Balella, "Sul riconoscimento giuridico dei sindacati," *Riv. Pol. Econ.*, XV (January 1925), 4–8, and Umberto Ricci, "Il sindacalismo giudicato da un economista," *Riv. Pol. Econ.*, XV (February 1925), 97–115. Also, De Felice, *Mussolini il fascista*, I, 691n.

had been considered silenced forever.[62] The strike also demonstrated that the Fascists could, if they chose to, make life difficult for all industrialists, a realization which undoubtedly helped to reconcile the industrial leadership to the idea of a Fascist *Gleichschaltung* of Italian society.

Neither side wanted to prolong the tension indefinitely. Having made their show of force, the Fascist leadership decided to hold out the olive branch. The minister of the interior, Luigi Federzoni, called in Benni and informed him that the government had decided that the CGII and Rossoni's Confederation of Syndical Corporations ought to work together more closely. Calm would be restored by making sure that strikes would be initiated in the future only as a desperate last resort. Benni informed the members of the CGII that no individual employer could declare a lockout in the future without the approval of the CGII.[63]

By April 1925, when Benni and Federzoni had their conversation, it was clear that the impending political reforms would not be as radical as the industrialists had anticipated earlier. The Commission of Solons was dominated by conservative Fascists. It followed Rossoni's wishes by recommending the elimination of non-Fascist syndical associations, but it did not specify what the function and power of the officially recognized Fascist associations would be. The syndical law of April 3, 1926 provided that only the officially recognized syndical associations had the right to conclude lawful labor contracts. The industrialists did not want to go that far but, on the whole, they could not be dissatisfied with the reforms recommended by the Commission of Solons. The reform essentially broadened the powers of the Head of Government and restricted those of parliament. It made the government more authoritarian and the industrialists had never objected to authoritarianism. They were concerned primarily with making sure that the new order developed with them rather than against them. They cooperated. In Benni's words, "An act of courage was therefore needed by which, overcoming all the absurd scruples that still manifested themselves

---

[62] CGII, *Annuario 1925*, p. 166. The strike is discussed in Franco Catalano, "Le corporazioni fasciste e la classe lavoratrice dal 1925 al 1929," *Nuova Rivista Storica, XLIII* (January 1959), 34–41. See, also, *O. I.*, April 1, 1925, p. 53.

[63] CGII, *Annuario 1925*, pp. 172–174.

here and there, we would break all contacts with non-Fascist organizations." [64]

The act of courage was performed when the CGII and Rossoni's confederation signed the Vidoni Palace agreement on October 2, 1925. Article 3 of the agreement specified that all labor contract negotiations would take place between the CGII and its affiliates on the one hand and the Fascist syndicates on the other. Non-Fascists labor unions were excluded from collective bargaining. The Fascist had to pay a price for this concession. The Vidoni agreement provided for the abolition of all workers' factory councils. That did not particularly displease the Fascists because most factory councils were still under Socialist control (a Socialist council had been elected by Fiat workers as late as September 1924), but Rossoni was angered when the CGII refused to recognize Fascist workers' trustees *(fiduciari di fabbrica)* with which he hoped to replace the factory councils. Benni insisted that the Vidoni agreement must broaden the authority of management. Mussolini made it clear that he agreed with Benni: "only the hierarchy of management should exist within the factory; therefore, we shouldn't even talk about trustees."[65]

The industrial leadership wanted to strengthen the authority of management within the factory and the authority of the CGII over individual firms. This was the message of a CGII circular issued a few days after the signing of the Vidoni agreement. Those industrialists who still did not accept the CGII were warned that their associations would be replaced by more cooperative ones.[66] Olivetti, who had been the most stubborn opponent of the Vidoni agreement, commented that "we must loyally admit that if the monopoly [over labor negotiations] represents a gain for the workers, it can also be advantageous for the industrialists and for the CGII." [67]

---

[64] *Atti. Camera,* 1929–1931, IV, 4532.

[65] *O. I.,* October 15, 1925, p. 145; September 1, 1929, p. 311. On the CGII's opposition to the introduction of factory trustees, see its *Circolare 442,* III, dated September 29, 1925.

[66] CGII, *Circolare 444,* III, dated October 10, 1925.

[67] *La Finanza Italiana,* XVII (October 10, 1925), 386. Curiously, these same words were used by Mussolini to justify the Vidoni agreement. See *Opera Omnia,* XXII, 43. Olivetti's apprehension about the possible consequences of Fascist totalitarianism for organized industry are evident in a letter of September 1924 to Mazzini who was then president of the Industrial League of Turin. Olivetti advised Mazzini that, should Mussolini decide to destroy the CGII, the

One thorny issue left unsolved by the Vidoni agreement concerned the introduction of compulsory arbitration of labor disputes. The government made it clear that it intended to ban strikes and lockouts on the ground that, as expressions of class interests, they failed to take into account national needs. Only officially recognized workers' and employers' syndicates were authorized to conclude labor contracts legally. To become the officially recognized syndicate, an association of workers or employers had to demonstrate its "capacity, moral acceptability, and national loyalty" to the satisfaction of government officials. Whenever these officially recognized syndicates failed to agree on the terms of a collective labor contract, the matter was settled by the compulsory arbitration of specially constituted labor courts.

The industrialists, who had accepted the Vidoni agreement with hesitation because they feared it might lead to more comprehensive regulation of labor relations, were determined not to yield on the question of compulsory arbitration. They began by raising specific objections designed to show the impracticality of compulsory arbitration. Could the government really guarantee the observance of arbitrated labor contracts? Were there enough competent arbitrators to staff the labor courts? Where were they to be found?[68]

When the matter came up for discussion in parliament in conjunction with the bill which eventually became the syndical law of April 3, 1926, Benni undertook the task of warding off compulsory arbitration. He attacked the principle of compulsory arbitration while the bill was still in committee. To overcome his stubborn resistance, the other members of the committee decided to grant his request that industry be specifically excluded from the jurisdiction of the labor courts. The battle was then transferred to the floor of the Chamber where Benni justified the exclusion of industry on the ground that no one but an experienced industrialist could judge the economic feasibility of a labor contract and stated unequivocally that the extension of compulsory arbitration to industry would mean economic chaos throughout the land.

---

industrialists should disband and abandon all political activity. The industrialists, although Olivetti does not mention it, actually concentrated all power in the hands of the CGII the better to resist Fascist totalitarianism. The letter is quoted in Abrate, *La lotta sindacale nella industrializzazione in Italia*, p. 426.

[68] *Riv. Pol. Econ.*, XV, (May 1925), 487–488.

There were obvious weaknesses in Benni's reasoning and Rossoni moved in to expose them. He pointed out that Fascist labor leaders were too aware of the real needs of production and too reasonable to make excessive demands. Benni was in an uncomfortable political position. If he persisted in his refusal to accept compulsory arbitration for industry, he would in effect be suggesting that he had no faith in the Fascist syndicalists, which could be construed as a slur on the entire Fascist regime. He rose to the challenge with tortuous verbal dexterity. Industry would accept any reform sponsored by the regime in the certainty that fascism could not possibly advocate anything contrary to the national interest. However, precisely because fascism stressed the importance of authority, order, and legality, industry could not approve of new agencies (the labor courts) which bypassed the authority of the state and undermined the basis of law and order. He concluded with the verbal somersault that the industrialists would follow Fascist directives "with daring prudence" *(con ogni audace prudenza)*.[69]

The lines were drawn and this time the industrialists were at a disadvantage. The opposition included not only most Fascists but also the representatives of agricultural and commercial employers who resented the special treatment demanded by the industrialists. Alfredo Rocco, the minister of justice who sponsored the bill and who had initially supported the industrialists, confessed that he was unhappy over the exclusion of industry from the jurisdiction of the labor courts. But the industrialists' most serious disadvantage was that this time Mussolini was not on their side. Their demands were so one-sided that Mussolini could not support them without antagonizing many followers and tarnishing the image of impartiality which he cultivated. He made his position quite clear:

I am not the secretary of the corporations but there has never been a major labor problem . . . which I have not examined and sometimes solved. Under the circumstances, I believe that the CGII can and will take this step, if for no reason than the advantages will outweigh the disadvantages.[70]

This time the industrialists had to yield. Industry had to accept

---

69 *Atti. Camera*, 1924–1926, V, 4888–4889.
70 *Ibid.*, 4960.

the principle of compulsory arbitration, although Olivetti was able to salvage a great deal. At his suggestion, parliament agreed that collective labor controversies should be reviewed by the highest syndical associations before being turned over to the labor courts.[71] This right of preliminary review gave the CGII the opportunity to settle most collective labor controversies outside the courtroom. By 1937, only forty-one collective labor controversies had reached the labor courts, only sixteen of which were settled by court decisions.[72]

The fact that the Vidoni agreement and the syndical law of 1926 were received by some industrialists with reservations cannot obscure the advantages which the industrial leadership derived from these measures. The CGII became the official and exclusive representative for all industrial employers vis-à-vis labor and government. We shall see in the next chapter how, as a result of this official recognition, the CGII extended and tightened its control over entrepreneurial groups that were still beyond its reach. It also entrenched itself more securely into the institutions of the Fascist state. As the official representative of industry, it was entitled to a permanent seat in the Fascist Grand Council, in government planning agencies, and after the parliamentary reform of 1928, in parliament itself. Furthermore, although the official recognition meant that the CGII would operate on a level of juridical equality with other employer associations and with labor syndicates, it exceeded the others in influence and prestige.

On the basis of the syndical law, workers and employers were organized separately in twelve national syndicates, one for each group in industry, agriculture, commerce, banking and insurance, land transportation and inland navigation, sea and air transportation. An additional association for professional workers, artists, and intellectuals brought the total to thirteen. The CGII was unquestionably the most powerful. After the government officially recognized it on September 26, 1926 as the exclusive representative of industrial employers, its new functions as a public agency complemented its continuing activities as a private pressure group. The industrialists continued to choose their own leaders who in turn ran the CGII without interference. Labor contracts concluded by

---

[71] *Ibid.,* 4964–4965.
[72] Aquarone, *L'organizzazione dello Stato totalitario,* pp. 133–136.

the CGII or its members were legally binding on all industrial firms. Freedom of contract was a thing of the past. Now the CGII enjoyed both the administrative autonomy of a private organization and the juridical authority of a public institution.

Juridically speaking, the syndical reform was a great innovation because it attenuated the traditional distinction between private and public institutions. In this sense, it approached one of the original goals of fascism. The CGII, however, remained the citadel of private business; it was nominally subject to the same government controls that applied to other syndical associations but, unlike them, it was strong enough to resist the demands of government officials and Fascist radicals. Organized industry was in the state but not of the state. The aspirations of revolutionary syndicalists, fascist revisionists, and integral nationalists were frustrated once again. All these groups envisaged a corporative state in which production was regulated by representatives of capital and labor organized side by side within the corporations where they would work together under the guidance of the state. The syndical reform assigned workers and employers to separate associations (the syndicates) which were authorized to deal only with labor problems. The enactment of the syndical reform meant that the realization of the corporative state was postponed indefinitely. The idea of corporativism was kept barely alive by a provision of the syndical law authorizing the formation of mixed associations of workers and employers, provided these mixed associations would not jeopardize the existence of the syndicates. The reasons for keeping the corporative principle alive will soon become apparent. The royal decree of July 1, 1926 which specified how the syndical reform was to be implemented also provided for the creation of a Ministry of Corporations and a National Council of Corporations. The presence of these two agencies enabled the regime to speak as if corporativism was already a working reality in spite of the fact that until 1934 there existed only one economically insignificant corporation for artists and intellectuals.

The concept of corporativism failed in 1926 for several reasons. The nebulousness of the concept strengthened those opponents who had specific objections. Olivetti was one of them. He opposed the corporations on the ground that the workers were allegedly still too immature and irresponsible to be given any say in the management of production (this was probably his way of saying that they were still under Socialist influence). He also feared that the establishment of mixed associations would mean the permanent removal of craftsmen and industrial cooperatives from the CGII.[73]

Only a few Fascists were seriously committed to the realization of the corporative state in 1926. Some integral nationalists and catholic intellectuals were committed to corporativism on intellectual grounds but lacked significant support in the party or in the country at large. Rocco, who of all former nationalists was perhaps most closely identified with fascism, was too much of an evolutionist and too sympathetic to big industry to insist on the enactment of meaningful corporative reforms at that particular moment. The one Fascist leader who put up a brave struggle was Rossoni but he was virtually isolated and was soon to succumb to a coalition of anti-Rossonian Fascists and to Mussolini's pent-up resentment of his growing power and prestige. For most Fascists corporativism was still little more than a slogan, a nebulous cause to which many paid lip service and few gave serious thought.[74]

Fascist ideologists began to differentiate clearly between syndicalism and corporativism after the syndical reform. Because the syndical state was an accomplished fact and corporativism could not be renounced, Fascist theoreticians had to devise a system that would give each a logical function. The most authoritative view, worked out by Bottai and endorsed by Mussolini, was that the two were complementary. Syndicalism was now declared to be a necessary pause on the way to the corporative state. Eventually, the syndicates would be absorbed by the corporative state thereby crowning the Fascist revolution.[75] All was sufficiently vague to serve several purposes. The distinction between syndicalism and corporativism now helped to prolong the myth of the continuing Fascist revolution and to justify the regime's ineradicable social ambiguity. Disgruntled Fascists who felt the syndical reform had not gone far

---

[73] *Atti. Camera,* 1924–1926, V, 4931–4936.

[74] Renzo De Felice, *Mussolini il fascista.* II. *L'organizzazione dello Stato fascista, 1925–1929,* (Turin: Giulio Einaudi, 1968), pp. 270–278.

[75] Giuseppe Bottai, *Esperienza corporativa (1929–1935)* (Florence: Vallecchi, 1935), p. 27, and *Opera Omnia,* XXIV, 216.

enough could look forward to the next round when the ambiguity would be dispelled.

Given its antecedents, the Fascist regime could follow no other course. Obviously, the distinction between syndicalism and corporativism was not the result of a spontaneous process of ideological clarification within fascism. Fascist social doctrines developed as they did because the regime was unable and unwilling to resolve its internal contradictions. Having come to power with the consent of powerful outside groups, fascism could hardly disregard their wishes once in power. The industrialists were the socio-economic force that resisted the revolutionary tendencies of fascism with the greatest success. Fascist economic and social reforms, therefore, were as much a product of industrialist caution as of the revolutionary aspirations of Fascist innovators. The industrialists were never strong enough to dominate fascism but they were always sufficiently influential to remain in the ring for the next confrontation. They accepted the syndical reform partly because it was a necessary step to strengthen the regime which to them was a necessary barrier to socialism, and partly because it was otherwise convenient for them to do so. The industrial leadership found the reform advantageous because it gave them new opportunities to discipline industry and because it gave them a better vantage point in the public administration from where they could continue to influence the course of Fascist reform and the formulation of public policy.

III

THE REWARDS OF PARTNERSHIP

Mussolini's assurance that the industrialists would gain more than they would lose from Fascist syndicalism may have been motivated by political expediency. Nevertheless, his words suggest that he had perceived a point that only the more politically sophisticated observers could appreciate. In their attachment to the traditional laissez-faire distinction between the public and private spheres, most industrial leaders did not readily grasp that by accepting a public role within the syndical state they would in effect expand the scope of private initiative. By giving business a formal role within the Fascist state, the syndical reform created the legal framework in which private and public initiative could eventually develop in complementary fashion.

Fascism did not originate the idea of a mixed economy. Private and public initiative had become interrelated in Italy and elsewhere long before the word fascism was fashionable. But fascism took the unusual step of trying to institutionalize the relationship between public and private power and in so doing, it followed a path different from that of the western democracies where the relationship developed in a more disguised form. In the final analysis, however, the difference was more in the form than in the substance with the Fascists shouting what the others, perhaps more wisely, preferred to whisper. The immediately noticeable consequence of giving private interests a public role within the syndical state was that these private interests could pursue their particular goals under cover of public policy.

The immediate effect of the syndical reform was to increase the regimentation and bureaucratization of both management and labor. Regimentation was not an accidental by-product of the syndical reform; rather it was the logical consequence of the regime's totalitarian aspirations. But although the aspirations were totalitarian the reality was not, partly because labor and management were regimented in different ways. As far as the letter of the law was concerned, both groups were subject to precisely the same discipline. In practice, however, the labor syndicates were run as extensions of the state bureaucracy by party-appointed officials while employer associations enjoyed effective autonomy under their own officials who were formally appointed by the government but who were responsible to their own constituents. This was particularly true of the CGII (the other employer associations in agriculture, commerce, banking, and transportation never enjoyed a comparable degree of autonomy). Organized industry emerged from the syndical reform as the most formidable business pressure group in the country even though the law gave the industrialists no special privileges. The CGII's highly effective formula for success was still that of flexible resistance, which the industrialists never abandoned although as time went on they had to stress the flexibility over the resistance. Their willingness to pursue the dialogue with fascism and their new status within the syndical state gave the industrial leaders the opportunity to assert themselves as sole spokesmen for all industrial employers from craftsmen to industrial magnates, to bargain with labor from a position of greater power, and to extend their influence as economic decision-makers.

REGIMENTATION IN INDUSTRY

The CGII was now officially recognized as the sole spokesman for industry. No industrialist could refuse to join it or to follow its directives without putting himself outside the law. The syndical reform legitimized the application of the Fascist principles of leadership and hierarchy within industry. To distinguish between those who joined only to fulfill their legal obligations and those who were full-fledged consenting members, the CGII introduced a dual-type membership. Firms that joined to be covered in collective labor contracts as specified by law belonged to the Syndical Section only; the full-fledged members joined the Economic Section as well. The first group was known as represented firms, the second as associated firms. Both paid membership dues (somewhat lower for the represented firms), thereby assuring the CGII a large and steady income. The fact that represented firms always outnumbered the associated ones (in 1938, to mention a typical year, there were 144,154 represented and only 87,125 associated firms) is a clear indication that many industrialists joined only to comply with the law.[1] Only fascism could give the industrial leadership that monopoly on representation that they had sought since 1919.

The compulsory enrollment of industrial firms was accompanied by a concentration of administrative power in the hands of CGII officials. The charter of 1926 gave the CGII the power of review and veto over all industrial associations. The president could appoint and dismiss their officials and control their finances. Labor contracts negotiated by industrial associations became effective only with CGII approval; the associations could not initiate any action before the labor courts without previous clearance. The CGII could effectively enforce discipline, including the suspension of duly appointed officials and the appointment of special caretakers sent from Rome (most top CGII officials served in this capacity at one time or another).[2]

Direct intervention in the internal affairs of industrial associations was, however, fairly uncommon. This customary self-restraint was part of a CGII plan to cultivate good relations with the membership whenever possible, a plan that also accounts for the retention of elective procedures in organized industry in spite of the fact that elections were contrary to the Fascist principle that all authority flows from above. Local businessmen were brought to Rome once a year to attend a national convention where they had an op-

---

[1] *O. I.,* July 1, 1938, p. 1.

[2] CGII, *Annuario 1928–29* (Rome: Cooperativa Tipografica Castaldi, 1929), pp. 251–253.

portunity to meet their leaders and establish useful contacts. The government never insisted that the industrialists abandon their elective procedures. Fascist radicals often complained that the industrialists were too independent but neither the government nor the party ever tried to put their own men in even minor posts within the CGII. With its autonomy and internal cohesion thoroughly protected, the CGII could deal with all outside interests from a unique position of strength. The industrialists' privileged position prompted Bottai to petition the Fascist Grand Council in November 1927 for a statement that all syndical associations were obliged to obey instructions issued by the Ministry of Corporations. Similar injunctions were repeated at frequent intervals with little noticeable effect on the industrialists.[3]

The CGII used its new authority to good effect. The independent printers saw their old association abolished in November 1926. They were subsequently organized in a new group that was headed by an outsider, the textile manufacturer Raimondo Targetti. Rumors of coercive enrollments were sufficiently widespread to elicit a warning from the Ministry of Corporations that all syndical officials should avoid giving the impression even in their private correspondence that the principle of voluntary membership was being flouted.[4] But the CGII was not primarily interested in chastising dissenters; it was more concerned with gaining representational control of large branches of production in the proximity of industry. Transportation firms, insurance companies, landlords, managers and business administrators, craftsmen, cooperatives, and public utilities were related to industry either as providers of services or as potential competitors. The industrialists were naturally eager to speak for them.

A major obstacle to the enrollment of these groups within the CGII was that other employer confederations in agriculture, banking, and commerce were also interested in them for similar reasons. The resulting controversies lasted in some cases for several years. Although the industrialists did not always prevail, they did well

---

[3] *Riv. Pol. Econ.*, XVII (November 1927), 946–947. Also, *O. I.*, February 15, 1931, p. 88; May 15, 1933, p. 274.

[4] *O. I.*, November 15, 1926, p. 170; February 15, 1927, pp. 37–41.

enough. Their losses included the insurance companies that went to the bankers and transportation firms that were organized independently until 1934 when they were finally assigned to the CGII. With these two exceptions, the industrialists had their way. The CGII took over the landlords on the questionable ground that anyone who operated any type of machinery in connection with his work or his property was to be classified as an industrialist; it incorporated public utilities in order to facilitate the solution of possible conflicts between public and private enterprise; it enticed business administrators and managers into joining for the sake of a more perfect union between capital and management, and even arrogated to itself the authority to distinguish between managers and plain laborers.[5]

A special word must be said about big industry's interest in the world of small-scale production consisting of craftsmen shops and cooperatives. Small firms operated in large numbers in all sectors of the economy. In industry, out of a total of 150,278 concerns registered in 1938, 107,126 employed ten workers or less—and in addition to these industrial firms there were 758,832 even smaller establishments classified as craftsmen shops.[6] Both small industry and the crafts were traditionally independent and suspected that enrollment in the CGII might be more in the interest of the larger firms that controlled the various trade associations than in their own. Efforts to organize small production by commercial groups and by Fascist syndicalists eager to gain a foothold among industrial employers were squashed by the CGII. When the question of the CGII's expansionism was raised in parliament by spokesmen for agriculture and commerce, Benni and Olivetti simply refused to discuss the matter in that forum. Olivetti cut off one deputy with a curt "don't concern yourself with these matters." [7]

---

[5] *Atti. Camera,* 1924–1925, V, 4945–4948. CGII, *Annuario 1930 – VIII* (Rome: Cooperativa Tipografica Castaldi, 1930), p. 341; *Annuario 1931–32 – X* (Rome: Cooperativa Tipografica Castaldi, 1932), pp. 262–266; *Annuario 1937 – XV* (Rome: Tipografica del Senato, 1937), pp. 253–254. Also, *O. I.,* October 15, 1930, p. 377; November 14, 1939, p. 1.

[6] CGII, *L'industria dell'Italia Fascista* (Rome: USILA, 1939), pp. 151, 161.

[7] *Atti. Camera,* 1924–1926, V, 4863, 4935–4936. Also, CGII, *Circolare 426,* III, dated June 11, 1925, and *Annuario 1925,* pp. 239–241.

The interests of large and small producers were sufficiently diverse to justify the small producers' lack of enthusiasm at the prospect of having to join the CGII. Small concerns enjoyed a flexibility in production schedules that they could use to great advantage against larger and therefore more routine bound competitors. Some small concerns engaged in highly seasonal work and could not adjust to the uniform wage scales and hiring practices prescribed by national contracts that were drawn up with the interests of large-scale production in mind. Small producers charged at various times that the larger firms were responsible for the failure of raw materials to reach their sector, for discrimination in the awarding of government contracts, and for inadequate credit and investment capital to sustain small-scale production.[8]

The small producer's plight in Fascist Italy stemmed in part from an unresolved contradiction of Fascist ideology. In an effort to reconcile modernization with the retention of traditional class structures, fascism entered into incompatible commitments. On the one hand, it promised to promote the concentration of ownership and management for the sake of greater efficiency. On the other, it vowed to protect the small producer against all encroachments. (Fascist art idealized the craftsman.) The presence of large numbers of small, independent producers was a challenge and a refutation of the Marxist dichotomy between capital and labor. The small producer was both employer and laborer, he related to his helpers in a highly personal way, he was proud of his skills, his finished product, and his humanity. The small producer was the very symbol of the integral society exalted by fascism.

Industrialists had a more prosaic view of the small producer. To the captains of industry the small independent producer was a nuisance whose presence complicated the operations of the industrial cartels that were designed to eliminate competition. At the same time, the larger industrial firms often found it advantageous to rely upon smaller concerns to provide them with a wide range of components and semifinished products. In the words of the secre-

---

8 CGII, *Annuario 1928–29*, p. 51. Also, *O. I.,* July 1, 1928, p. 175; January 21, 1937, p. 1; March 18, 1937, p. 5; July 29, 1937, p. 3; September 9, 1937, p. 1; February 3, 1938, pp. 1–2; May 19, 1939, pp. 5–6; July 18, 1939, p. 1; July 25, 1939, p. 1.

tary of the Federation of Craftsmen, "the craftsman does not always work for the public. On the contrary, he receives his orders largely from industrialists or, more frequently, from dealers." [9]

While fascism idealized the small producer as the embodiment of the dignity and independence of labor, powerful economic interests were bent on regulating him to a subordinate position as a supplier of needed services and goods. The conflict was resolved with a typical "Mussolinian" compromise. The CGII was authorized to distinguish between craftsmen and small industrialists; it decided promptly that firms with five or more workers be classified as industrial establishments and enrolled in the regular industrial associations where, inevitably, they would have to conform to the policies formulated by the dominant groups. This meant that wages, working hours, hiring practices, welfare provisions and countless other matters were settled with scant regard for the special needs of the small producer.

Firms with fewer than five workers were classified as craftsmen shops and organized in a Federation of Craftsmen that enjoyed autonomy within the CGII. The arrangement was not liked by many groups of small producers. Tailors complained that the separation of the larger from the smaller firms disrupted a natural community of interests. Nor were the craftsmen as autonomous as they would have liked to be. Labor contracts negotiated by the regular industrial associations were binding on industrialists and craftsmen alike. Craftsmen often complained that they had won formal organizational autonomy at the cost of economic independence. Their grievances were voiced in impassioned terms by their president, Vincenzo Buronzo:

... it should be understood that the craftsmen must be equipped with all the mechanical devices provided by science. . . . We want to compete, we want to be tested against you industrialists, and if there are mechanical devices . . . that will sustain our creativity, our unique inventiveness, if we can utilize what science provides, you must recognize that such devices and machinery have their place in the craftsman's shop.[10]

---

[9] Mario Baruchello, *Politica dell'artigianato* (Rome: Società Editrice di Novissima, 1935), p. 45. Also, CGII, *Annuario 1931–32*, pp. 910–912, and *Il Sole*, March 24, 1935, p. 1.

[10] *O. I.*, October 15, 1930, pp. 377–378.

Cooperatives were initially denied even that measure of protection that Fascist ideology gave to the crafts. Business and fascism had launched their attack against the cooperatives in the immediate postwar period when cooperatives had proliferated thanks in part to extensive public subsidies. In some cases, particularly in agriculture, cooperatives had developed into large establishments that competed successfully against private concerns. Cooperatives had often been attacked by the Fascist *squadre* supported and instigated by resentful landowners who looked upon cooperativism as being economically subversive. After the March on Rome the fight against cooperatives was waged by legal means. Some 2,000 cooperatives were forced to shut down when public subsidies dwindled; by 1930 there were only 3,300 consumer cooperatives in existence. Many of these were cooperatives in name only, as it seems that they had been taken over by individuals who ran them for personal gain.[11]

By the time the syndical reform was enacted, cooperativism was no longer a threat to private initiative. The CGII was therefore more interested in preventing the resurgence of cooperativism as a large-scale phenomenon than in carrying out a pointless vendetta against surviving cooperatives. Because the future of cooperativism would depend in good measure on the official status of cooperatives within the syndical system, advocates and opponents of cooperativism argued at length about their placement. Those to whom cooperatives were a legitimate type of business organization that fascism might eventually want to encourage argued that cooperatives should have their own independent national association. Others felt that cooperatives were not entitled to special treatment and that they should take their place with other employers in the regular associations in agriculture, commerce, or industry. Had the latter view prevailed, cooperativism might well have disappeared as a concept in Fascist Italy. Mussolini knew, however, that a complete rejection of cooperativism was politically inexpedient at a time when the government tried to curb the rising cost of living. He was quick to recognize cooperatives as being in the interests of consumers. The government and the CGII agreed that cooperativism should not be an issue. The way was therefore open to a

---

[11] Rosario Labadessa, "Il bilancio della cooperazione di consumo in Italia," *Riv. Pol. Econ.*, XXIII (March 1933), 296–302.

compromise that would satisfy both the government's commitment to protect the consumer and the CGII's desire to prevent conflicts of interest between cooperatives and regular industrial firms. The final decision incorporated a suggestion made by the economist Gino Arias and supported by Olivetti to the effect that cooperatives should have their own independent National Bureau of Cooperation but that their trade associations should also join the regular employer confederations. The National Bureau would enjoy full administrative autonomy and would be solely responsible for welfare provisions within the cooperatives. At the same time, being under the jurisdiction of the employers' confederations, the cooperatives would have to conform to prevailing labor, production, and pricing policies.[12]

As had the craftsmen, cooperatives won the form but lost the substance of independence. The CGII openly admitted that its qualified acceptance of cooperatives rested on the fact that "having abandoned once and for all its original intentions, Italian cooperativism no longer represents or wants to represent a tendency toward a new system of production." [13] In other words, cooperatives could continue to function as long as they did not compete with regular firms, a qualification that destroyed an essential function of cooperatives and denied Mussolini's own premises for accepting cooperativism. It is no accident that, after 1935 when the regime began to look upon cooperatives with greater favor and decided to gove them the full autonomy that had been denied to them a decade earlier, the CGII showed little enthusiasm and insisted that the number of cooperatives be kept at a minimum.

The syndical reform extended the Fascist principle of leadership among businessmen to a degree that would have been inconceivable in an open society. But regimentation in Fascist Italy often was not what it seemed to be. According to the syndical law, all official associations were subject to higher authorities, in the case of the CGII these being the Ministry of Corporations and, ultimately, the *Duce*. Mussolini, however, exercised his authority only when important political issues were at stake, while the Ministry was inadequately

---

[12] For Mussolini's views on cooperatives, see *Opera Omnia*, XIX, 10–11; XXII, 173–174. For the Arias motion, see *O. I.*, October 15, 1930, p. 379.

[13] CGII, *Annuario 1930*, p. 366.

staffed. Individual firms were regimented by their superiors in the CGII rather than by party or government officials. The chain of command that the syndical reform strengthened within industry did not customarily cross the crucial junction where private interest meets public authority. Considering that a similar situation existed in most public agencies, ministries, local administrations, party precincts, and even the secret police, we will understand that the average Italian was often at the mercy of middle and high-level manipulators of power who were seldom responsible to someone else. What made life difficult in Fascist Italy was not so much the rigidity of the law as the arbitrary use of power.

There was one important exception to the disjunction of public authority and private power. Labor was subject to a chain of command that extended without interruptions from the *Duce* to the humblest worker.

THE REGIMENTATION OF LABOR

On social reform, the regime walked a tightrope: it could neither disregard its promises of far-reaching changes nor could it afford to alienate its conservative backers by fulfilling those same promises. Accordingly the regime needed a labor leadership endowed with an exceptional political sensitivity and disposed to bend to political realities. To be effective within the system, or simply to survive in power, Fascist labor leaders had to be vocal but not intemperate, inspire confidence in both labor and business, and be loyal to both their working class constituents and to the party. As all leaders who must respond to conflicting demands, they satisfied none. Businessmen and conservative Fascists accused them of being crypto-Socialists while workers dismissed them as tools of the bosses.

Not many people met all the stringent prerequisites. The man who probably met them least of all was Rossoni. As long as Fascist labor unions had to compete against Socialist and catholic rivals, Rossoni's radical past and his rhetorical aggressiveness were valuable assets. The syndical reform and the elimination of non-Fascist organizations changed the situation. Mussolini now needed more docile labor leaders and started to vent his resentment of Rossoni. In September 1927 when Rossoni stated publicly that the regime had failed to lower the cost of living after having applied extensive wage cuts, Mussolini peremptorily ordered him not to address public rallies until further notice. The *Duce,* by that time, had at his disposal a large dossier on Rossoni's personal and political peccadilloes and was ready to use it at the opportune moment.[14]

The industrialists had their own reasons for resenting Rossoni. More than the man, they feared his organization. All labor groups in every sector of the economy were united under Rossoni's leadership while the employers were organized in six separate confederations. Labor was united whereas business was fragmented. Although Rossoni's lack of support within the party made it unlikely that he could ever use his monopoly to good effect, business felt at a disadvantage in labor negotiations. The CGII therefore demanded the *sblocco* (busting) of Rossoni's General Confederation of Fascist Syndicates into six autonomous confederations in symmetry with those of business. After a protracted wrangle in which Rossoni was abandoned even by sympathetic revisionists like Bottai, Mussolini forced Rossoni's resignation in December 1928. His resignation coincided with the *sblocco* of the labor movement precisely as the CGII had requested. From then on, the CGII dealt with the Confederation of Fascist Industrial Syndicates as its exact counterpart in labor was now called. Business no longer had to worry about a potentially formidable association of all workers.[15]

Labor leaders sought to obtain compensation for the *sblocco* by introducing the workers' trustees within the factory that the industrialists had rejected at the time of the Vidoni agreement. The Fascist Federation of Metal Workers actually announced early in 1929 that it would appoint such trustees regardless of how the employers felt about it. The CGII then intervened promptly with a direct message to Mussolini that businessmen could not be held responsible for the course of production if the authority of management within the factory was diminished. Mussolini agreed with the industrialists who commented gratefully: "Once again, the *Duce* has exercised his magic power to clarify the situation and restore

---

[14] Rossoni knew that Mussolini was waiting for the favorable moment to dismiss him. Cianetti told him as much in a letter dated March 22, 1926, now in *Archivio Centrale dello Stato* (Rome), *Carteggi di Personalità,* Cianetti collection, folder B-8.

[15] On Rossoni's forced resignation, see Carmen Haider, *Capital and Labor Under Fascism* (New York: Columbia University Press, 1930), pp. 214–215.

trust and serenity to our minds." [16] Workers' trustees were not introduced until 1939 when a changed political situation gave labor leaders their long sought opportunity.

The labor movement entered the great depression of the 1930's in disarray and frustration. Deprived of the right to strike and of the confidence of workers, labor leaders sought to retain some credibility by resorting to infighting and backstairs politicking, thereby becoming ultimately dependent on Mussolini, and giving him that central role which he had not always had with Rossoni in charge. Pietro Capoferri, who understood the situation fully, refused to accept an appointment as head of the Milanese labor syndicates until Mussolini had personally reassured him of his unqualified support.[17] But as Mussolini usually moved by cold political calculus, labor had to wait for the proper political climate to develop before achieving significant breakthroughs. The Fascist labor movement lacked the independence to pursue its own coherent, long-range plan to gradually increase labor's share of the national wealth. It was possible for labor to obtain concessions provided its leaders knew how to take advantage of favorable opportunities. There was little that labor could do, however, to help create those opportunities. The record of the Fascist labor movement must be judged in the light of the fact that its leaders could respond but not initiate.

Within these limits labor leaders could do several things. They could exploit those provisions of the syndical law that guaranteed a collective labor contract to every trade and occupation. If properly enforced, collective contracts could provide uniform wages and fringe benefits, thereby reducing the possibility of arbitrary decisions by individual employers. However, enforcement was the real problem. Employers got around the provisions of collective labor contracts by introducing machinery or labor saving techniques that extracted more work without a commensurate pay increase.[18] Appeal procedures were cumbersome enough to discourage the formal expression of all but the most serious grievances. The

---

[16] CGII, *Annuario 1930*, p. 998.

[17] Pietro Capoferri, *Venti anni col fascismo e con i sindacati* (Milan: Gastaldi, 1957), pp. 48–51.

[18] For a discussion of how labor saving techniques were used against labor, see Paola Fiorentini, "Ristrutturazione capitalistica e sfruttamento operaio

labor courts rarely reviewed such complaints, which did not prevent the various interest groups from working to have their own men appointed to the courts. The CGII insisted that labor judges be chosen among managers and businessmen rather than civil servants, academicians, or experts in labor relations whose knowledge of the problems of production was said to be too bookish to be of practical value. Although we do not know as much as we should about the labor courts, the CGII's views must have prevailed because it declared itself satisfied over the appointment of industrial candidates as labor judges. In spite of this, the CGII continued to block recourse to the labor courts because it claimed that the settlement of labor disputes was best left to those who had practical knowledge of production.[19]

Generally workers and labor leaders felt that employers were guilty of frequent breaches of contract. Their numerous complaints soon caused a huge backlog in the labor courts because the charges were hard to substantiate and the courts were inadequately staffed. Industry and labor agreed eventually to bypass the labor courts entirely and settle the controversies through bilateral negotiations. This procedure apparently expedited settlements but, at the same time, it also removed these cases from the only forum where they could be disposed of under public scrutiny.[20]

Wage settlements illustrate more clearly the restrictions of Fascist syndicalism. Because many labor leaders originated from the party, their loyalty was divided between the party and the labor movement. There was always tremendous pressure on them to behave like party members first and labor leaders second. They were vulnerable to charges that they might be more sensitive to class than to national interests, a charge that would have pleased most non-Fascist labor leaders. Employers were therefore on strong ground when they could plausibly argue, as they always did, that wage reductions were in the interest of the national economy. The general

negli anni '20," *Rivista Storica del Socialismo,* X (January–April 1967), 149–150. Also, CGII, *Annuario 1930,* pp. 999–1001; *Annuario 1931–32,* pp. 686–689; *Annuario 1933 – XI* (Rome: Tipografia del Senato, 1933), pp. 808–809. Also, *O. I.,* February 24, 1934, p. 1.

19 CGII, *Annuario 1928–29,* pp. 451–452; *Annuario 1930,* pp. 782–783, 790–791; *Annuario 1931–32,* pp. 705–707.

20 Capoferri, *Venti anni col fascismo,* pp. 156–159.

reduction of October 1927, ranging from ten to twenty percent of current wages, was presented as an inevitable consequence of the government's battle to protect the purchasing power of the lira. The wage cuts of December 1930 (8 percent) and May 1934 (7 percent) were justified by business as necessary steps to keep Italian exports competitively priced in order to improve the nation's unfavorable balance of trade. In all instances, labor leaders obeyed party orders, thereby indicating that the decision was reached at the political level rather than at the bargaining table. Negotiations primarily were designed to satisfy public opinion and followed a familiar pattern: management would ask for an unrealistically high wage cut, labor would make a low counteroffer, and party officials would then mediate until the two sides met somewhere in the middle. Management was thus given an opportunity to manifest its reasonableness, the labor syndicates to demonstrate their usefulness, while the party (or Mussolini) emerged as the guardian of the national interest. The workers probably missed the fine points but they were in no position to express their feelings.

Labor leaders had to wait for the general political and economic situation to change before they could recover the losses. The situation changed after 1935 as increased military spending resulted in higher prices and Italians were called upon to face the hardships of war. Labor now pressed its case by using the same national interest argument used earlier by business. According to the most reliable study, increases negotiated between July 1936 and March 1939 raised wages to the 1928 level. Because the wages of 1928 already reflected the cuts of 1927 as well as the sizable unofficial reductions of earlier years, it seems certain that by 1939 wages had not regained their pre-Fascist level.[21]

The strategy of the Fascist labor leaders was to seek supplementary compensation in the form of fringe benefits and social security programs. Their achievements along these lines were by no means negligible. The programs that were either initiated or expanded included paid vacations, compulsory severance pay, special end-of-the-year bonuses, free legal assistance for workers who sought a re-

---

[21] Cesare Vannutelli, "Le condizioni di vita dei lavoratori italiani nel decennio 1929–39," *Rassegna di Statistiche del Lavoro,* X (May–June 1958), 97–108.

dress of grievances from their employers or wished to apply for social security benefits, special factory funds to assist disabled workers, disability and unemployment insurance, subsidies to workers with large families, public drives to stamp out such widespread afflictions as malaria and tuberculosis, special care for mothers and infants. The most popular innovation was probably the *Opera Nazionale Dopolavoro* established in 1925 to provide recreational facilities, organize group excursions and cultural events at popular prices. Although the *Dopolavoro* was established and run by the party, it was turned over to the labor syndicates in October 1939 over the protests of the CGII which was suspicious of anything that might make the labor syndicates popular among the workers.

The industrialists reasoned it was more important that the workers develop a sense of loyalty toward their employers than toward class organizations.[22] They were fond of quoting Mussolini's well-known comment that intelligent capitalists do not concern themselves only with wages but also with housing, schools, hospitals, and recreation for their workers. In line with this paternalistic image, the CGII supported a number of philanthropic projects such as free clinics for the care of tubercular workers. The larger industrial firms often ran cut-rate stores for their employees. Unfotunately, such projects dwindled drastically as soon as the economic depression began to cut into profits. Philanthropy failed at the moment when it was most needed.

The government stepped into the void. The intensification of public assistance in the 1930's was an inevitable consequence of the economic depression and of the regime's commitments to both labor and management. An objective observer easily perceives that, in the manner of all welfare societies, the regime moved to provide those public services without which private initiative could not continue to function. Few industrialists, however, would accept this line of reasoning. To them, money spent on public assistance was money diverted from productive investment. As businessmen elsewhere, Italian industrialists rarely wavered in their conviction

[22] CGII, *Annuario 1928–29*, pp. 640–641.

that the best way to combat the depression was for the government to provide direct assistance to private initiative while leaving the free market to take care of labor and consumer. They were more interested in what was happening at the supply than at the demand side of the market.

While the industrialists often claimed credit for the regime's welfare programs, they worked behind the scenes to limit their scope and reduce their cost. As employers were usually expected to share the cost (and always complained that their share was too high), the CGII successfully demanded a voice in the administration of most welfare programs. CGII representatives won numerous concessions for business. Among other things, they were able to convince the Ministry of Corporations that the burden of proving that an employer had failed to comply with welfare regulations should rest on the worker and that employers were not obliged to provide proof of compliance.[23]

The industrialists were suspicious of welfare programs more for what they indicated about the regime's intentions than for what they actually provided. They feared that the regime's expanding social commitment would lead to an infringement of managerial prerogatives. They were determined to protect managerial power within the factory. When the government decided in 1928 to establish state employment offices in the various provinces, the CGII made sure that they kept only rosters of unemployed workers from which management could choose whenever it wished to fill a vacancy. Management remained basically free to hire and dismiss at will.

Labor gained a small voice in factory management only in 1937 when workers' representatives were admitted to boards authorized to develop wage classifications and set piecework compensation rates. This innovation, and the already mentioned introduction of workers' trustees in 1939, were enough to create the uneasy feeling among businessmen that the regime was becoming too radical.

INDUSTRY AND THE ADVENT OF
THE CORPORATIVE STATE

The industrialists' determination to protect managerial authority affected the corporative reform that had been postponed *sine die*

---

[23] CGII, *Annuario 1931–32*, pp. 686–689.

by the syndical compromise of 1926. We have already seen that the Ministry of Corporations was set up without the corporations. The corporations had remained a vague reference in Article 3 of the syndical law to the effect that the syndicates might be linked by means of "central connecting agencies" staffed by representatives of labor and management. None was actually set up because, as Benni and Olivetti explained in the Chamber, management could not agree to giving the workers a voice in production.[24]

Subsequent steps to realize the corporative state stopped short of seriously challenging the authority of management. The Charter of Labor promulgated by the Fascist Grand Council in April 1927 was hailed in Fascist circles as the Magna Charta of the Fascist revolution. In reality, there was little in that document to justify the claim. In its final form, the charter reflected a compromise between the CGII and Rossoni, with the industrialists gaining most of their points. Business interests in all sectors of the economy joined forces under Benni's direction to make the charter a statement of general principles rather than specific provisions on wages, working hours, fringe benefits, and social security as Rossoni would have preferred.

The industrialists' battle was more than half won once it was decided that the charter would be issued in the form of a general social manifesto. When it came to phrasing the charter, Benni argued that it must assert the "purely Fascist principle" that every individual has a specific function in society and that "the function of the industrialist is to organize and manage production." [25] He won his point but not as fully as he would have preferred. The charter promised respect for managerial independence but also stated that management was ultimately responsible to the state which could regulate production whenever the public interest required it to do so. The ambiguity was absolutely necessary. Since the regime had to satisfy both traditionalists and innovators, to clarify that point would have meant disrupting the social balance that sustained the regime.

As the pressure to clarify the meaning of corporativism increased in the early 1930's, the industrialists lost no opportunity to thwart

---

[24] *Atti. Camera,* 1924–1926, V, 4931–4934.

[25] See Benni's interview in *Il Popolo d'Italia,* March 19, 1927, p. 2. For a discussion of the Charter's background, see De Felice, *Mussolini il fascista,* II, 286–296.

the plans of those Fascists who still hoped that something qualitatively new might emerge from the Fascist revolution. The most radical expectations were voiced by a professor of philosophy at the University of Rome, Ugo Spirito, during a well publicized colloquium that took place in May 1932 in Ferrara. Spirito defended the daring proposition that private property should be abolished and that ownership should be vested in the Fascist corporations. Such "proprietary corporations" would then assume full responsibility for production, thereby putting an end once and for all to the historical conflict between private and public interest.

It is not surprising that the revolutionary implications of Fascist doctrine should have been enunciated by an academic intellectual. Everyone involved in the realities of power was too busy manipulating and compromising to follow Fascist postulates to their revolutionary conclusions. Olivetti, who participated in the Ferrara colloquium, rejected Spirito's suggestions in no uncertain terms. But even Bottai, who had a reputation for intellectual independence and who favored the evolution of a new system of property relations, felt Spirito had gone too far. Specifically, Bottai rejected Spirito's contention that the corporations should supersede the syndicates. He had opposed Rossoni's brand of syndicalism on the ground that it exasperated those class antagonisms that fascism was supposed to transcend. Now that the labor syndicates were under more moderate leadership, Bottai felt they had a useful role to play. He argued that as long as capital and labor retained any vestige of their class mentality, the separation of workers and employers simply reflected a fact of life.[26]

On this last point, Bottai and the industrialists were in agreement. Business had learned to live and work with the syndical system and had little desire to take another leap in the dark. The decision, however, was not up to them. Fascism could not afford to renounce the myth of the continuing revolution. To halt its progress, particularly at a time when most Fascists felt the need for some spectacular gesture to deal with the economic depression, would have ended the complicated give-and-take that held the regime together. Most industrialists therefore resorted once again to the well-tested strategy of flexible resistance. The one industrial-

---

[26] Aquarone, *L'organizzazione dello Stato totalitario,* pp. 198–201.

ist who went too far in opposing the new experiment was Olivetti and his intransigence cost him his post as secretary of the CGII (Mussolini forced his resignation in December 1933). Probably exhausted by years of hard work, and increasingly antagonistic toward Mussolini whose demagogic, plebeian ways clashed with his austere self-restraint, Olivetti at the Ferrara colloquium committed the blunder of expressing his opposition to the principle of corporativism. Most of his colleagues worked quietly but effectively to limit the regulatory power of the corporations over production. They insisted that corporative agencies have purely advisory functions, that they respect the legislative prerogatives of parliament, that labor negotiations remain in the hands of the syndical associations, and that all corporative decisions be subject to review by Mussolini. The twenty-two corporations that were finally established in 1934 conformed to all these criteria.[27] In July 1932, probably to reassure the industrialists, Mussolini took over the Ministry of Corporations from Bottai.

But the industrialists were not simply interested in rendering the corporative experiment harmless, they also wanted to use the corporations to facilitate the restructuring of the system of production to their greater satisfaction. One of the specific functions of the corporations was to promote cooperation between the different sectors of production. Benni agreed that this would be highly beneficial: "Our vision of the economy is a Fascist vision, an integral vision; agriculture, banking, and commerce stand at industry's side." [28] Most corporations covered large cycles of production. The corporation for textiles included the agricultural groups that produced the fibers, the manufacturers who processed them, and the commercial organizations that marketed the finished product. Other corporations, such as those for building construction, machinery, chemicals, and public utilities included only industrial and commercial groups. The arrangement was designed to reconcile

[27] The steps whereby the industrialists obtained satisfaction on most demands may be followed in *Atti. Camera,* 1929–1930, II, 1627–1628, 1652–1653; 1929–1931, IV, 4533–4534. Also, *O. I.,* January 31, 1931, pp. 41–42; September 15, 1933, p. 500; December 15, 1933, p. 722. For a description of the structure and functions of the corporations, see William G. Welk, *Fascist Economic Policy* (Cambridge: Harvard University Press, 1938), pp. 121–133.

[28] From Benni's speech to the annual convention of industrialists sponsored by the CGII, in *Riv. Pol. Econ.,* XVIII (June 1928), 559.

the need for economic planning with the desire of the various economic groups for some autonomy.[29]

We need to examine now why the industrialists preferred the corporative approach to economic planning. Their attitude toward corporativism can hardly be understood without taking into account the impact on their thinking of the great economic crisis that followed the crash of the American stock market in October 1929. The effects of the crisis were not immediately evident in Italy because the Italian economy was already experiencing a recession due to the deflationary policy adopted by the government after 1925. Apologists for the regime, including numerous industrialists, took advantage of this coincidence to boast that a Fascist economy was immune from the cyclic disturbances of capitalism. When the period of grace proved to be shortlived, the government began to experiment with various forms of economic interventionism in a flurry of poorly coordinated moves strongly reminiscent of the early days of Roosevelt's New Deal.

The industrialists were now faced with a serious dilemma. They could not afford to refuse public assistance, nor did they want to risk public regulation of production by accepting public assistance. Their aim was as clear as it was difficult to achieve: to have public assistance without public regulation. Their reaction was therefore both bold and oblique. On the one hand, Benni called upon the industrialists to save themselves by adopting labor saving techniques, scientific management, and rationalization of production. On the other, he asked for a massive infusion of public funds into the private sector to rescue the firms that were on the verge of bankruptcy.[30] The idea was to justify keeping control of production in private hands in spite of industry's need for large-scale public subsidies by showing that industry was still sufficiently strong and vital to clean its own house.

---

[29] There was considerable debate over the structure of the corporations. The final compromise was apparently worked out under Mussolini's personal supervision. In addition to the cycle corporations mentioned, there were other single-trade corporations. See *O. I.*, September 15, 1933, p. 499; September 30, 1933, pp. 529, 533; October 31, 1933, pp. 607–608; November 15, 1933, pp. 643–650; January 13, 1934, p. 1.

[30] *L'Informazione Industriale*, November 27, 1931, p. 2, and *Riv. Pol. Econ.*, XXII (February 1932), 195–200.

Government responses to the crisis included the vast subsidies Benni had called for. The public rescue of private initiative was carried out by the *Istituto per la Ricostruzione Industriale* (IRI), a government agency set up in January 1933 to provide financial assistance to industrial firms, which we discuss in the next chapter. At this point we should mention that although in the long run it was IRI that changed the character of the Italian economy, the industrialists were initially more worried about other forms of economic interventionism. Much to Benni's chagrin, there were many influential Fascists who argued that the government should intervene directly to encourage the concentration of ownership and management and the rationalization of production. The idea was not new. Industry and government had worked together to rationalize production since the mid-1920's. One reason why the industrialists had supported Mussolini's policy of monetary deflation after 1925 was that they hoped a temporarily declining level of profits would drive many marginal producers out of business to the advantage of the larger and supposedly more efficient firms. But deflation could not be pushed beyond a point without the risk of driving every producer into bankruptcy. That point was reached in 1927 when Mussolini decided to stabilize the currency at his famous *quota 90* (to be precise, at the exchange rate of 92.46 lire to the pound sterling) against the advice of many businessmen who feared that stabilization at such a high exchange rate would entail a drastic loss in exports.[31]

After business had accommodated itself with some difficulty to *quota 90,* it looked as if further changes in the structure of production would have to be initiated by direct public intervention, which most industrialists wished to avoid. In the government, Belluzzo and Bottai were in favor of industrial cartels as a way of reducing fragmentation of ownership and management. The idea was taken up by Arnaldo Mussolini, the dictator's influential brother, who argued that producers should be required by law to

---

[31] The industrialists' commitment to a deflationary policy and monetary revaluation is discussed in Roland Sarti, "Mussolini and the Industrial Leadership in the Battle of the Lira, 1925–1927," *Past and Present,* No. 47 (May 1970), 97–112. The industrialists' opposition to stabilizing the currency at *quota 90* is emphasized in De Felice, *Mussolini il fascista,* II, 246–258.

join cartels whenever total participation was in the national interest. The suggestion was unacceptable to industry for a number
of reasons. To have such government sponsored *consorzi obbligatori*
(compulsory cartels) would be an admission that the industrialists
were incapable of managing production efficiently without outside
leadership. The very principle of the separation of private and
public initiative was at stake. There was widespread fear in industry that compulsory cartels would pave the way to complete public
regulation of production. Benni therefore rejected the idea in no
uncertain terms in spite of the fact that Arnaldo Mussolini was
generally known to speak for his brother.[32]

The industrialists wanted to save the principle that cartels should
rest on the voluntary participation of their members even though
they were prepared to admit that compulsory cartels might be desirable under exceptional circumstances. Not only did voluntary
cartels reduce the risk of public regulation, they were also a convenient means of regulating competition. Of course, voluntary cartels seldom led to significant improvements in the methods of production. They usually took the form of price agreements whereby
prices were pegged at a sufficiently high level to assure the survival
of even the least efficient producers.[33]

Ironically, the CGII was instrumental in promoting passage of
a law that authorized the government to form compulsory cartels.
In spite of its formal stand in favor of voluntary membership, the
CGII was always ready to favor compulsory cartels on pragmatic
grounds. When the leading firms in steel insisted that the particular
needs of their sector made it imperative that all producers belong
to cartels, the CGII agreed with them. In fact, the CGII appealed
to the government to prevail upon a few nonparticipating firms to
join two sales cartels. Having intervened successfully, the govern-

---

[32] On the controversy between Benni and Arnaldo Mussolini, see *Il Popolo
d'Italia*, April 8, 1930, p. 1, and April 15, 1930, p. 1.

[33] In the absence of adequate economic analysis, it is difficult to generalize
about the cartels' impact on the structure of production. Most observers agree
that they did not promote rationalization or improve productivity to any significant degree. For general comments along these lines, see Rosario Romeo,
Breve storia della grande industria in Italia (Rocca San Casciano: Cappelli,
1963), pp. 158–160. For an interesting case study, see Tullio Ortu Carboni, "La
concorrenza nell'industria meccanica," *Riv. Pol. Econ.*, XXIII (February 1933),
164–171.

ment felt the need to legitimize its intervention by passing an appropriate law. Bottai argued in parliament that because many industrialists frequently disregarded the principle of voluntary membership in practice even as they upheld it in principle (and he mentioned names and instances when strong-arm tactics had been used to coerce individual firms into joining), it was incumbent upon the government to make sure that cartels were run in the national interest.[34] The law on compulsory cartels passed in June 1932 but the CGII saw to it that it remained a dead letter. When the two steel cartels expired in February 1933 they were renewed on a voluntary basis with the participation of all firms, an indication of the CGII's suspicion regarding compulsory cartels.[35]

There was the possibility that those who favored public regulation of production might seize upon the proliferation of voluntary cartels as an excuse to demand more stringent controls over production. The industrialists needed a legal umbrella that would legitimize the regulation of competition on the basis of private price and production agreements between businessmen. They found that umbrella in corporativism. They discovered the usefulness of the corporative principle of the *autodisciplina delle categorie* (collective self-regulation by businessmen within the various corporations). Now that the ubiquitous cartels curtailed the independence of managers at the factory level, the industrialists preferred to talk about collective rather than individual self-regulation. Leading business and political personalities argued that the corporations were fascism's answer to capitalism and socialism and that the practice of collective self-regulation within them struck a happy balance between the atomism and unpredictability of free market economies and the bureaucratic inefficiency of centralized systems.[36] This rhetoric cannot obscure the fact that corporativism was a useful smoke screen to disguise the retention of economic power in private hands.

[34] *Atti. Camera,* 1929–1932, VI, 6765–6766.

[35] The brief history of the steel cartels is discussed in ASIA and CGII, *Relazione sull'attività degli Uffici economici (28 novembre 1932 – XI)* (Rome: Cooperativa Tipografica Castaldi, 1932), pp. 75–77, and CGII, *Annuario 1933,* pp. 464–468.

[36] *Opera Omnia,* XXVI, 150, 356. Also, Pirelli's speech of October 15, 1934 to the general assembly of the CGII in *Riv. Pol. Econ., XXIV* (September–October 1934), 954–963.

As most of the twenty-two corporations cut across several sectors of production, it naturally made it easier for previously competing groups to reach mutually acceptable agreements. Although the activities of the corporations have not been studied in sufficient detail, there are indications that they served the industrialists' purpose. One-third of the cartels registered in 1937 were formed after the enactment of the corporative reform. Manufacturers, landowners, and commercial dealers discovered the advantages of coordinating their pricing and marketing policies. Agrarian-industrial cartels included those between beet growers and sugar refiners, producers of textile fibers and textile manufacturers, dairy farmers and manufacturers of dairy products. The best example of an industrial-commercial cartel is the sales cartel in cotton formed in June 1932 between several thousand manufacturers and dealers. In March 1934 this cartel was authorized by the government to assign fixed quotas of raw materials to its members, to determine how much each participant should produce, what share of the market he was entitled to, and at what prices he should sell. When in April 1936 these powers were extended to all cartels provided they would submit to the Ministry of Corporations an annual statement of their activities, the cartels became the regulators of production. Decision-making powers were taken away from local managers and vested instead in the business elites that represented the dominant firms. Because the cartels always assigned raw materials, production and market quotas on the basis of a firm's past share of the market, the proliferation of cartels acted as a powerful brake on the entire economy. Acquired positions were perpetuated and newcomers excluded from the market. As a result, there were large numbers of small firms struggling to emerge, confined to a gray zone of semi-legality, at the mercy of bureaucrats, and whose workers were underpaid, insecure, and beyond the reach of social security programs.[37]

---

[37] CGII, *Annuario 1937*, pp. 661–666. The figures given by the CGII probably fall far short of the actual number of cartels in operation. According to the law on cartels, a voluntary cartel could be based on an unregistered verbal agreement among the participating firms. For a description of the major industrial-commercial cartels, see Confederazione Nazionale Fascista del Commercio, *Commercio 1922 (I) – 1932 (X)* (Rome: Confederazione Nazionale

The corporative agencies supposed to supervise the work of the cartels could never do so effectively. The staff of the Ministry of Corporations was overwhelmed by the avalanche of reports from the numerous cartels. When the corporations began in 1935 to take over the task of supervision, their investigating boards discovered that the reports were not sufficiently detailed to make the investigations meaningful. The investigators also discovered that supplementary data was difficult to come by even though they were authorized by law to request all necessary clarifications. When the corporation in steel and machinery decided after hearing numerous complaints to look into the activities of some forty cartels that were nominally under its jurisdiction, its investigators were unable to reach any conclusion on the basis of the information available. The fact that workers and employers had equal representation on the boards of the various corporations meant that debates could go on indefinitely if either side was determined to stall for time.[38]

The failure of the corporative state to establish effective controls over the cartels reveals how Fascist totalitarianism functioned in practice. The industrialists were fond of describing the cartels as totalitarian, perhaps as a semantic effort to disguise their coercive basis. The cartels, however, were totalitarian only in the sense that they severely restricted managerial autonomy at the factory level. They were not totalitarian in the sense that they disciplined private power in the public interest, however that elusive concept may be defined. The corporative principle of the *autodisciplina delle categorie* as practiced by the cartels was ultimately incompatible with the regime's totalitarian aspirations. The incompatibility became clear as soon as the regime tried to mobilize the country's natural and human resources for war. With that effort, we move into the

---

Fascista del Commercio, 1933), pp. 403–405. References to other important cartels appear in *O. I.*, April 31, 1931, pp. 242–248; June 30, 1932, p. 380; July 15, 1932, p. 402; July 31, 1932, pp. 439–441; September 15, 1932, p. 359; March 10, 1934, p. 1; August 11, 1935, p. 1; January 16, 1936, pp. 1, 5.

[38] *O. I.*, June 28, 1938, p. 1. Labor leaders were often critical of the lack of public controls on the cartels. See Pietro Capoferri, "La posizione dei consorzi nell'economia corporativa," *L'Economia Nazionale*, XXX (September 1938), 4–5. For penetrating comments on the functions of the cartels, see Giulio Scagnetti, *Gli enti di privilegio nell'economia corporativa italiana* (Padua: CEDAM, 1942), pp. 226–231.

period of autarky, or the pursuit of economic self-sufficiency, as a
necessary prerequisite to a more independent foreign policy.

THE REGIMENTATION OF PRODUCTION
IN THE PURSUIT OF AUTARKY

It would be misleading to explain the policy of autarky simply in
terms of domestic developments. Most countries became more protectionist and exclusivist during the economic crisis of the 1930's.
But autarky became an official policy only in the countries where
economic and political power was concentrated in the hands of
elites willing to sacrifice the short-run economic advantages of international trade for the sake of long-run political objectives. Among
these countries, however, Italy was a special case. While in the
Soviet Union political and economic leadership was one, and in
Germany and Japan the political or military element was dominant,
the Italian industrial leadership was still sufficiently independent
of party and government to bargain with them from a position of
relative power.

Under normal circumstances, Italian industrialists would not
have been in favor of a policy of autarky. Their desire to protect
the domestic market always had to be balanced against their inescapable dependence on imported goods. Even the most successful
program of autarky could not possibly compensate for the natural
scarcity or nonexistence of coal, oil, metal ores and numerous other
products in the national subsoil. The industrialists therefore stood
somewhere between ultraprotectionist agrarian interests and doctrinaire free traders, although closer to the former. In the early
1930's Guarneri fought a successful two-front battle against both
groups. To the agrarians who favored a system of "balanced exchanges" that would have curtailed both imports and exports drastically, Guarneri replied that the economically advantageous course
for national production was for industry to buy whatever it needed
wherever it was cheapest. Benni supported him by pointing out
that industry would be happy to increase its purchases of Italian
agricultural products provided Italian farmers would sell at competitive prices. To the argument that the best way to end the economic depression was to create a European free-trade area, Guar-

neri replied that in such an area Italy would soon become an agrarian client-state of the more industrially advanced nations.[39]

The first inducement to rely more heavily on domestic resources was financial. Italian exports declined by nearly two-thirds between 1929 and 1935 because of new protectionist measures adopted by other countries and because of the government's failure to devaluate the lira in proportion to the devaluation of the pound sterling in 1931 and the American dollar in 1933. The decline worsened the chronically unfavorable balance of payments, draining the country of its reserves of precious metals and foreign currencies that guaranteed the stability of the lira. Bankruptcy was averted only because imports fell between 1929 and 1935 by nearly as much as exports. By February 1935 imports were subjected to a system of licensing that greatly inconvenienced industry and, as we shall soon see, became a source of constant friction between industry and government. The more difficult it became to obtain industrial supplies from abroad, the more Italian manufacturers had to rely on domestic substitutes. One consequence of this situation was that industry and agriculture drew closer in a new symbiotic relationship that manifested itself in the formation of numerous agricultural-industrial cartels. The severe restrictions on imports also led to the mining of extremely low-grade ores in the national subsoil that could not have been exploited economically in a less protectionist environment.

But the decisive considerations that pushed the Italian economy into a policy of full-fledged autarky were political rather than financial. Mussolini declared that autarky was an official goal only after the League of Nations imposed economic sanctions against Italy soon after the attack on Ethiopia in October 1935. Autarky now took on powerful emotional overtones. It is always risky to generalize about popular feelings but it seems certain that Fascist propaganda convinced most Italians that the policy of autarky was nothing less than a test of the national will to assert itself in the face of economic sabotage from abroad. In this supercharged atmosphere, the industrialists could hardly voice whatever reservations

[39] Guarneri, *La politica degli scambi con l'estero,* pp. 18–19. Also by Guarneri, "Contro la tregua doganale," *Riv. Pol. Econ.,* XX (February 1930), 113–117. Benni's comments appear in the same issue of *Riv. Pol. Econ.,* 181.

they may have felt about the economic wisdom of autarky. The industrial press endorsed the policy of autarky with unrestrained enthusiasm.[40]

Unfortunately for the regime, nationalistic fervor could not compensate for the defects in the bureaucratic machinery available for the implementation of autarkic goals. The corporative principle of the *autodisciplina delle categorie* was one of the first casualties in the battle for economic self-sufficiency. Twenty-two separate corporations, scores of assorted corporative bureaus, and several hundred cartels operating on the principle of self-regulation were bound to interfere with the mobilization of the nation's resources. The realization that autarky and corporativism were incompatible was not slow in surfacing. By 1938 even the minister of corporations, Ferruccio Lantini, admitted publicly that the policy of autarky would succeed only if the regime abandoned the principle of self-regulation.[41]

Understanding, however, does not always produce a cure. The regime found it politically expedient to pursue the policy of autarky with the cumbersome machinery of the corporative state. The corporative bureaucracy had become a powerful vested interest that was determined to perpetuate itself. Business groups were now accustomed to operate through the cartels and the corporations and were actually using them for additional tasks such as the implementation of price controls, the regulation of trade and of private investments. The habit of compromise and makeshift solutions was so ingrained in Mussolini that he could hardly escape it now although he became increasingly resentful of the restrictions of the system. Rather than admit that the corporative experiment was a failure, an admission that would have been politically embarrassing, Mussolini decided to superimpose new agencies on the existing

---

[40] The issue of *O. I.*, November 18, 1937, is a good example of how the industrialists glorified the policy of autarky. Industry's autarkic achievements are emphasized in Giuseppe Volpi, "Autarchìa industriale," *L'Economia Italiana*, XXIII (May 1938), 398–403.

[41] *O. I.*, June 24, 1938, p. 1. For Mussolini's views on the need for economic planning, see *Opera Omnia*, XXVII, 241–248. Mussolini's *piano regolatore* was much talked about after 1935 but no one could describe it with any precision. A good example of the fuzzy thinking that passed for economic analysis in the period of autarky is Luigi Lojacono's *L'indipendenza economica italiana* (Milan: Hoepli, 1937).

ones. The industrialists approved and perhaps even encouraged his decision not to bypass the corporative machinery. Apparently Volpi suggested to Mussolini that the Central Corporative Committee be enlarged and transformed into the *Commissione Suprema per l'Autarchìa,* the agency with overall responsibility for the implementation of autarkic goals.[42] The resulting maze of intersecting bureaucratic channels and overlapping jurisdictions made it easier for organized business to retain control of production regardless of the pressure from other quarters for public regulation and centralization.

The combination of autarky and bureaucratic inefficiency had an impact on the structure of production that in many cases survived the fall of the Fascist regime. The economic wastefulness of the combination was perhaps less significant in the long run than the fact that it gave unprecedented economic power to the larger producers who used the bureaucratic machinery created by the regime to consolidate their respective positions on the national market. Through this machinery, established producers gained even from the most direct forms of economic interventionism practiced by the Fascist government such as the attempts to regulate industrial expansion and trade.

Even the most well intentioned aspirations of Fascist planners were frustrated and perverted once they filtered through the bureaucratic maze. This was the case with the policy of "industrial licensing," practiced on a gradually expanding scale only after 1933, although the first steps in that direction had been taken as early as 1927. The policy was intended to prevent wasteful duplication of industrial investments but its results were quite different. The new policy enabled the industrialists to regulate competition more effectively, establish *de facto* monopolies, and curtail production at a time when many firms already operated at reduced capacity. Conti, Olivetti, and others stressed that the time had come to curb speculative investments even at the risk of hampering the work of some respectable producers.[43]

To accomplish their purpose, the industrialists had to control

---

[42] *O. I.,* October 21, 1937, p. 1; February 3, 1938, p. 1. For a description of the many agencies involved in planning for autarky, see Ferruccio Lantini, "Gli organi dell'azione autarchica," *Politica Sociale,* XI (May 1939), 185–187.

[43] *Atti. Camera,* 1929–1932, VI, 7583–7588. Also, *O. I.,* April 15, 1933, p. 204.

the licensing process whereby individual firms were authorized to make industrial investments. The responsibility rested officially with the Ministry of Corporations whose staff was neither large enough nor technically qualified to evaluate the numerous applications. The CGII was therefore authorized to receive and evaluate the applications and to pass them on to the ministry with its recommendations. A special committee within the ministry then made the final decision. Although the activities of this committee have not been studied because the documentation is not available, it has been suggested that it acted as a rubber stamp for the CGII. The CGII's influence apparently increased after January 1937 when the authority to make final decisions was vested in the corporations.[44]

Responsibility for the implementation of the policy rested therefore primarily with the CGII which was reticent about this aspect of its work. Partial data provided by the CGII indicates that the major beneficiaries of the licenses were the chemical, steel, machinery, and textile industries, in that order of preference. The fact that the number of applications grew in rough proportion to the proliferation of cartels indicates there is a connection between the regulation of industrial investments as practiced by the CGII and the consolidation of acquired positions in production.[45]

The evidence indicates that the larger firms took advantage of a loophole in the law regulating industrial investments to secure some lucrative monopolies. The penalty for constructing or expanding an industrial plant without permission or for failing to act upon a granted license was a 10,000 lira fine, a relatively small sum considering what could be at stake. Once a license was issued, government officials most likely rejected similar applications in order to prevent unnecessary duplicate investments. A firm could

---

[44] Gualberto Gualerni, *La politica industriale fascista (1922–1935)* (Milan: Istituto Sociale Ambrosiano, 1956), pp. 56–60. Also, Antonino Santarelli, "La disciplina corporativa delle nuove iniziative industriali," *L'Economia Italiana,* XXIII (November 1938), 927–930.

[45] CGII, *Annuario 1937,* p. 684. Also, *O. I.,* January 14, 1937, p. 1; July 15, 1938, p. 1; November 7, 1939, p. 1. See, also, Antonino Santarelli, "Dati e considerazioni intorno alla disciplina corporativa delle nuove iniziative industriali," *Rivista Internazionale di Scienze Sociali,* XII (January 1941), 63–64, and by the same author, *La disciplina degli impianti industriali* (Padua: CEDAM, 1947), p. 16.

look upon the 10,000 lira fine as insurance against competition. The fact that of 5,114 licenses issued between 1933 and 1940 only 414 had resulted in actual investments by the end of the Second World War, when licensing was discontinued, is an indication that many industrialists used licensing to consolidate positions of privilege.[46] Once again, self-regulation meant that private and public interests were working at cross purposes.

The regulation of trade practiced on a vast scale after February 1935 produced similar results. Mussolini moved Guarneri from the directorship of the CGII's economic services and put him in charge of regulating imports. Holders of foreign currencies were requested to deposit their reserves with the Bank of Italy. Guarneri then assigned foreign currencies to the various cartels, which in turn assigned them to the various firms for the purchase of necessary supplies abroad. The foreign currencies were assigned on the basis of a firm's past share of the traffic of imports, creating a tendency to freeze the various producers at their existing capacity. A select group, thirty of the largest firms, was singled out for special treatment by being granted fixed quotas that assured them a steady supply of iron and steel.[47]

The adoption of severe import restrictions, however, marks a special transitional moment in the relationship between business and government. With most developments associated with autarky,

[46]These figures are cited in Rossi, *Padroni del vapore e fascismo*, pp. 225–226. The abuses of the licensing system were denounced by Pietro Capoferri, "Limiti e funzioni della legge sugli impianti industriali," *Gerarchìa*, XVII (December 1937), 835. According to the head of the Fascist secret police, a lively traffic in industrial licenses developed even in Mussolini's secretariat. See Guido Leto, *OVRA, fascismo, antifascismo* (Rocca San Casciano: Cappelli, 1951), pp. 151–153.

[47] *O. I.*, May 12, 1939, p. 5. The list of privileged firms included Ansaldo, Ilva, and Terni in steel, Snia Viscosa in the production of synthetic fibers, Fiat, Montecatini, and *Porto di Venezia*. This last business corporation provides an excellent textbook case for ecologists. It was set up by Volpi who loved his native city of Venice and wanted to restore economic viability to a town that had been economically stagnant since the sixteenth century. His project backfired in a tragic way. The many industrial plants that operate around Venice today, through Volpi's initiative, are constantly draining fresh water from the city's subsoil, with the result that the city now threatens to sink gradually and disappear into the lagoon that surrounds it.

the industrialists had always obtained adequate compensation for
the economic inconveniences that they incurred. There was little
that the government could do to compensate them for the loss of
vitally needed supplies, particularly since the import quotas for
1935 sometimes ranged from only ten to thirty-five percent of the
monetary value of imports in 1934. The CGII did not hide its dissatisfaction with the restrictions. Senator Giorgio Enrico Falck of
the steel industry criticized the restrictions in the Senate, although
he was careful to say that he recognized the national need for
them.[48]

With the adoption of severe trade controls, the country reached
the delicate point where political considerations intruded immediately and directly upon the conduct of economic affairs. Trade
controls were extended to all sectors of the national economy because of the severe strain that the war against Ethiopia and the intervention in the Spanish Civil War placed on the treasury. The balance of payments deficit in 1937 was a staggering 3.5 billion lire.
The financial strain might have been alleviated had Mussolini been
willing to pursue a more conciliatory foreign policy, but that
was precluded by his determination not to risk a loss of political
prestige.

The industrialists had supported fascism on the assumption that
under Mussolini's pragmatic leadership it would not seriously
challenge their control of production. Until the late 1930's, they
had little reason to suspect that it might be otherwise. Though
Mussolini had occasionally displayed a curious stubbornness, these
instances could be dismissed as little more than momentary aber-
rations. The industrialists had gone along with the policy of autarky
in spite of its obvious economic drawbacks mainly because they
were carried along by the wave of nationalism that swept across the
country during the war against Ethiopia and because the economic
sacrifices of autarky were offset by gains. Autarky and corporativism
brought previously conflicting business groups together in a network of cartels that was the economic expression of the *union sacré*
sealed under the banner of aggressive nationalism. In the sense
that autarky gave every established interest group a place in the

---

[48] *Atti. Senato*, 1934–1935, I, 1046.

economy commensurate to its achieved status and past performance, autarky was a triumph for economic conservatism. Autarky eliminated the social mobility and opportunities for economic expansion that perhaps would have been possible in a less regimented economy but, at the same time, guaranteed every established producer or combination of producers a fixed share of the market and an acceptable though probably not spectacular level of profits.

In the closed system, the industrialists, the large landowners, the Church, the bureaucracy, and even the vast middle class of shopkeepers, craftsmen, and small peasant proprietors enjoyed the psychological satisfaction of knowing that they had a definite place and function in the national economy. Labor, always a potential source of movement and unrest in such a system, was securely regimented and perhaps even partly reconciled to the loss of its freedom by the rewards, however modest, of an incipient welfare state. The social atmosphere was permeated with that sense of permanence that comes of immobility, the reassurance of knowing what one owes to one's neighbor that often comforts economically senescent societies. Nostalgic Italians still regret the loss of that sense of identity and kinship even while they deplore the modest material standards or outright deprivations that they experienced under the Fascist regime.

An expansionist foreign policy was bound to change all that. One is tempted to describe the regime's expansionism as an attempt to infuse movement and energy into a social and economic system that tended to settle into stagnant routine. We must now examine how the industrialists reacted to this new situation. There is reason to believe that, like many other sensible Italians who only wanted to be left alone to do their work, the industrialists had dismissed the regime's bellicosity as a publicity stunt. Even the Ethiopian War may not have alarmed them unduly because it was waged against a minor power in a fairly remote part of the world. In any case, most Italians perceived that venture more as a settling of old scores and as the fulfillment of a perfectly legitimate colonial mission than as an act of wanton aggression. But the subsequent political alliance with Nazi Germany, military intervention in Spain, and Mussolini's growing ambition to play a major role on the world scene raised some troubling new prospects. At that point, the industrialists had to confront the political in addition to the purely economic implications of the policy of autarky. Businessmen who had never really internalized the warlike ethic of fascism soon discovered that, in their determination to mobilize the country for war, the Fascist leaders were ready to hedge on the unspoken terms of their partnership with business: the politicians challenged the autonomy of business as they had never done before.

IV

THE LIMITS OF PRIVATE POWER

The regime's political and economic oligarchies originated, respectively, from the two groups that constituted the initial social basis of fascism: the political activists of lower middle class extraction who provided the leadership and most of the manpower for the Fascist *squadre,* and their business supporters who supplied most of the funds.[1] The two groups joined forces before the March on Rome for essentially negative reasons: resentment of the growing power of blue-collar workers, disillusionment with liberal governments that seemed incapable of restoring law and order, fear of "creeping socialism." They were never united by positive affinities.

The alliance of these two groups was never free of tensions. Perhaps the most surprising thing about the Fascist regime is that it survived long after its promoters had achieved their initial goals. The alliance was prolonged on the unspoken assumption that

---

[1] An awareness of the mixed social basis of fascism is evident in Gramsci's early writings on fascism. See *Opere di Antonio Gramsci.* XI. *Socialismo e fascismo. L'Ordine Nuovo, 1921–1922* (Turin: Giulio Einaudi, 1966), pp. 297–299. See, also, Palmiro Togliatti's essay of 1928, "A proposito del fascismo," now in Costanzo Casucci, ed., *Il Fascismo. Antologia di scritti critici.* (Bologna: Il Mulino, 1961), pp. 279–301.

neither side would trespass on the other's territory. Fascist leaders felt that they were accountable to no one in the exercise of their political functions while business leaders, often suspicious of everything that smacked of politics, claimed that they were the only ones with the necessary qualifications to manage and direct production.

Such a division of functions was fairly easy to maintain in the absence of major economic or political crises. The 1930's witnessed many economic and political crises. Consequently, during that decade the understanding between the economic and the political leadership was subjected to new and fairly severe strains. The economic depression forced business leaders to ask the government for financial assistance while the Fascist drive to mobilize the country for war necessarily meant more politically motivated demands on business. The traditional laissez-faire distinction between the economic and political spheres seemed irrelevant if not positively undesirable under these new conditions. The industrialists understood this well but they also feared the possible loss of their organizational independence and basis of power which they had protected so well in the course of other confrontations with the politicians of the regime.[2]

Mussolini had been the industrialists' best ally in previous years. Unlike Hitler who was driven by an irrepressible sense of mission that made him a compulsive initiator, Mussolini behaved essentially as a political mediator devoted to preserving the balance of forces that supported his regime. Depending on the circumstances, he strengthened this or that current, distributed his support to this or that group with considerable shrewdness, sometimes tactfully, sometimes ruthlessly. His detractors called it his unprincipled opportunism and his admirers his consummate sense of politics. With

---

[2] We are not suggesting that there was no interpenetration of the economic and political oligarchies. There were Fascist leaders who occupied government posts that gave them considerable say in economic matters just as there were businessmen who held important political posts. Particularly in the 1930's, businessmen, politicians, and civil servants often sat together in the same government planning agencies as demonstrated by Louis Rosenstock-Franck. *Les étapes de l'économie fasciste italienne; du corporatisme à l'économie de guerre* (Paris: Librairie Sociale et Economique, 1939), pp. 44–46, 274–277. It is nevertheless clear that the conduct of foreign affairs rested entirely in the hands of Mussolini and a select number of political advisers. The industrialists neither gained nor, as far as we know, ever sought admission to that group.

his manipulative talents, he gained for fascism the support of powerful outside interest groups, including the industrialists, and tied these groups to one another and to the party in a system of checks and balances, spheres of influence, concessions, and compensations that contrasted sharply with the regime's monolithic facade.

Granted that the industrialists were attracted by Mussolini's political pragmatism, it is difficult to explain their enduring faith in the man. Many had become "Mussolinians" before the March on Rome and remained so even after it became clear that Mussolini's attitude toward them was changing. His often noticed awe of businessmen who understood the intricacies of production and finance so much better than he did was also mixed with a feeling of contempt for what he sometimes sneeringly described as the "bookkeeper's mentality." The industrialists were slow to grasp that in Mussolini's scale of values politics always came before economics. He was willing to let the businessmen run production and make economic decisions so long as their actions conformed to his political goals. The priority of politics became obvious during and immediately after the Matteotti crisis when he allowed the Fascist syndicalists to disrupt production with numerous strikes in order to pressure the industrialists into accepting his constitutional reforms. His indifference to economic considerations emerged during his campaign to stabilize the lira at *quota 90* in 1927. To the industrialists and to his own minister of finance who argued that stabilization at such a high exchange rate would be bad for business, Mussolini replied stubbornly that *quota 90* was necessary to protect the regime's political prestige. Olivetti, of all industrialists probably the one least convinced of Mussolini's reliability, commented on that occasion "that man . . . is really capable of killing all of us by bringing the exchange rate to five lire to the dollar."[3] Few of his colleagues drew similar conclusions.

Observers who argued that there was no room for "economic man" in a Fascist society were not entirely mistaken.[4] What they

---

[3] Oreste Mosca, *Nessuno volle i miei dollari d'oro* (Naples: E. Scarfoglio, 1958), p. 225. For Volpi's objections to *quota 90* we have Guarneri's testimony in *Battaglie economiche*, I, 159. Conti spoke out against *quota 90* in his Senate speech of May 21, 1927. See *Atti. Senato*, 1924–1927, VII, 8202–8216.

[4] The classic example of this type of interpretation of fascism is Peter F. Drucker, *The End of Economic Man* (London: W. Heinemann, 1939).

did not emphasize sufficiently was that Fascist indifference to economic calculus manifested itself only under exceptional circumstances. There was certainly no disregard for economic convenience during the early years of the regime. With the revealing exception of *quota 90*, fascism continued to give business almost everything it wanted until the mid-1930's. We have already seen that businessmen were adequately compensated for the economic sacrifices they had to sustain due to the policy of autarky.

Fascism approached a crossroad when the momentum of politically motivated exactions on business began to exceed the government's ability to extend proportionate compensations. Compensations began to fall short of exactions as a result of general economic and political developments over which neither the business leaders nor politicians had full control. The international economic depression threatened to drive major financial and industrial establishments into bankruptcy, compelling private enterprise to rely heavily on public subsidies. As a result of the depression, businessmen could no longer claim that the private sector of the economy was self-sustaining; they had no choice but to accept the rise of a mixed economy in which private and public enterprise were inextricably linked. Economic difficulties and the simultaneous corporative reforms in the early 1930's encouraged the Fascist leadership to seek a solution to the economic crisis and the fulfillment of the Fascist revolution by political means in the area of foreign affairs. Conditions were ripe for Mussolini to vent, finally, his hitherto repressed ambitions for political and territorial aggrandizement. The rise of public enterprise and political expansionism were the two new developments of the late 1930's that threatened to disrupt the established *modus vivendi* between business and fascism.

THE RISE OF PUBLIC ENTERPRISE

Fascism did not initiate the practice of using public funds to subsidize private businesses. The first step in that direction was taken in December 1914 when the Italian government helped to set up a consortium to finance industrial development and war production. The first major rescue operation occurred in 1921 when the same consortium was allowed to draw heavily on treasury funds to avert the financial collapse of two interlocking establishments, Ansaldo and the *Banca Italiana di Sconto.* In 1923 Mussolini's government went a step further when it intervened to save the *Banco di Roma.* In the period 1914–1923 government loans to industry amounted to 5.7 billion lire. The government also found itself saddled during those years with depreciated industrial securities that were nominally worth 3.3 billion lire that neither the banks nor individual investors were willing to buy.[5]

The government undertook these rescue operations for a number of reasons. In the case of the *Banco di Roma,* Mussolini was eager to please Vatican authorities who were interested in that bank. But the government's motivations were of a more general nature. Industrial establishments the size of Ansaldo obtained government aid because they employed thousands of workers who would become unemployed if their firm went bankrupt and because they produced armaments and equipment that were necessary for national defense.

In the case of the banks, there was an additional reason. No government could ignore the need to protect personal savings and, in Italy, small depositors were usually among the first victims of economic recessions. German financiers operating in Italy in the 1890's had introduced a type of bank that engaged in both short-term commercial and long-term industrial credit. The banks always invested a high proportion of the money deposited with them in industrial loans and securities. The practice encouraged industrial expansion. Unfortunately, it did so at the expense of those who could least afford the inevitable risks. When small depositors went to withdraw their savings in times of crisis, they often discovered that the money was not there; it was tied up in long-term loans and in industrial securities that the banks could not dispose of quickly without incurring serious losses. The banks' inability to reimburse depositors spread panic among broad segments of the population that otherwise would not have been directly affected by a business crisis. At such times, the government had no choice but to rescue

---

[5] Constantine E. McGuire, *Italy's International Economic Position* (New York: Macmillan, 1926), p. 505.

the banks at public expense in order to prevent greater social and economic dislocations.[6]

When the government came to the aid of a bank, it usually took over its holdings of assorted securities as a form of collateral. This was done during the business recession that accompanied the stabilization of the lira at *quota 90*. The same thing, but on a larger and more systematic scale, was done during the early years of the world economic depression. The CGII itself asked the government to intervene as soon as it became clear that the banks could not take up the large quantities of industrial securities that investors and speculators were unloading on the market. Benni informed the executive council of the CGII in November 1931 that he was about to present to the government a plan for the systematic subsidization of private initiative. Similar requests were also made subsequently by other prominent industrialists, including Conti and Volpi.[7]

The government responded immediately by setting up the *Istituto Mobiliare Italiano* (IMI) which was authorized to collect both private and public funds for the rescue operations. When IMI's endowment of 500 million lire turned out to be insufficient, the government decided to rely solely on public financing through the already mentioned *Istituto per la Ricostruzione Industriale* (IRI) that was set up in January 1933. IRI's appearance was not surrounded by the publicity and fanfare that accompanied many far less important innovations. It took on the job in a subdued and businesslike manner that gave no indication of the enormous impact it was destined to have on the Italian economy.[8]

IRI's initial obscurity is easily explained. The industrialists

---

[6] On the banking system, see Francesco Parillo, "Stato banchiere, politica creditizia, sviluppo economico," in *Studi in onore di Epicarmo Corbino* (Milan: Giuffrè, 1961), pp. 602–607.

[7] *L'Informazione Industriale*, November 27, 1931, p. 2. *O. I.*, April 15, 1933, p. 204. See, also, Pietro Grifone, *Il capitale finanziario in Italia* (Rome: Giulio Einaudi, 1945), p. 194. The bankers were as eager as the industrialists to obtain public subsidies but subsequent suggestions by industrial leaders that the banks were solely responsible for industry's predicament should be taken with a grain of salt. See Senator Vittorio Cini's speech of April 1, 1935 in *Atti. Senato*, 1934–1935, I, 1024–1027.

[8] The most extensive description of IRI appears in Ministero dell'Industria e del Commercio, *L'Istituto per la Ricostruzione Industriale, I.R.I.* Vittorio

assumed that it would "simply wither away" as soon as it had done its job and returned the rescued concerns to private ownership. In Conti's words, public financing was to be just a temporary phenomenon to sustain private initiative as long as prices kept falling "and not to replace it—as some would have it—with direct [public] control and management of production."[9] The bankers, who were more preoccupied than the industrialists about IRI, could not object to its demands because of their obvious inability to help the industrialists in their hour of need. The *Banca Commerciale Italiana,* with about four billion lire tied up in industrial securities (three-quarters of its total assets) was the bank that stood to lose the most by having to surrender its holdings to IRI. Its director, Giuseppe Toeplitz, tried hard to protect the bank's interests but, in the end, had to resign himself to surrendering the bank's holdings to the government.[10]

Mussolini was careful not to antagonize the businessmen unnecessarily by appointing to IRI anyone associated with the syndical or corporative currents of fascism. The men who took charge of IRI were capable technicians of no noticeable political color. The man he chose to head IRI, however, may not have been as apolitical as he pretended to be. Alberto Beneduce, who presided over IRI from its inception until November 1939, was a most remarkable personality. His technical qualifications were beyond question. He had made a name for himself as a statistician interested in problems of finance, insurance, and population during the first decade of the century when the study of statistics was most neglected in Italy. After a fling at university teaching, he had plunged into politics as a moderate Social Democrat and had served in various capacities, including a brief stint in 1921–1922 as minister of labor and welfare under Premier Ivanoe Bonomi who was as moderate a Social Democrat as Beneduce. At the time of the March on Rome, Beneduce had scurried here and there trying to convince people that fascism

---

Ugo Ristagni, ed. (Turin: Unione Tipografico-Editrice Torinese, 1955–1956), 3 vols., particularly Volume III, *Origini, ordinamenti e attività svolta,* written by Pasquale Saraceno. A brief discussion of IRI's origins appears in Mario Einaudi, Maurice Bye, and Ernesto Rossi, *Nationalization in France and Italy* (Ithaca: Cornell University Press, 1955), pp. 196–200.

[9] *O. I.,* April 15, 1933, p. 204.

[10] Conti, *Dal taccuino di un borghese,* p. 466.

should be suppressed by force. He continued to oppose fascism until Mussolini eliminated the political opposition after the Matteotti crisis. At that point, Beneduce decided to withdraw from public life and devote himself to a career in business. Thanks to his expertise, his administrative ability, and his friendship with important business personalities, including Volpi, and Bonaldo Stringher, who was the governor of the Bank of Italy, Beneduce went straight to the top in record time. Of his numerous posts on the boards of directors of several business corporations, the most important was probably the presidency of the *Società per le Strade Ferrate Meridionali,* a holding company that controlled the electrical sector.[11]

Beneduce might have reached the conclusion that a career in business would give him the opportunity to play that public role that had been denied to him in politics. As a business director, he carefully avoided identification with political currents and issues. He made his way back into political circles by relying on his technical qualifications. Mussolini, who was greatly impressed by Beneduce's competence and apparent personal loyalty, often turned to him for advice. Beneduce thus handled for Mussolini many technical problems related to the stabilization of the currency in 1927. There were conservative Fascists who never overcame their suspicion of Beneduce for his unorthodox personality and past political affiliations but Mussolini and the industrialists held neither against him.

Beneduce, like Mussolini essentially a technician of power than an ideologue, found his position as head of IRI congenial with his inclinations. His relish for power and his sense of independence were fully gratified. He was accountable only to Mussolini who did not usually concern himself with the highly technical problems of production and finance that IRI dealt with. Beneduce wielded his power in an indirect way that had the advantage of protecting him from direct attack by his critics and of minimizing friction with the business leadership. There were many opportunities for such fric-

---

[11] A useful biographical sketch of Beneduce appears in the *Dizionario biografico degli italiani.* Beneduce's personality and techniques are discussed briefly in Alberto De Stefani, *Baraonda bancaria* (Milan: Edizioni del Borghese, 1960), pp. 558–561, and Eugenio Scalfari, *Storia segreta dell'industria elettrica* (Bari: Laterza, 1963), pp. 75–86.

tion to develop because Beneduce used the powers of IRI to revamp the entire system of production.

Although Beneduce never theorized about the changes that he proposed to introduce, he could not resist the temptation to hint broadly about the existence of a *piano Beneduce* for the economy. Given his reticence, the scope of the plan must be inferred from what actually happened rather than from what was said or written. Beneduce took advantage of the general economic improvement that came during 1935 to put an end to IRI's lending activities. As of March 1936 IMI took over all subsidizing operations. At the same time, the government ordered the banks to refrain from extending medium and long-term credit to industry and limit themselves to short-term commercial loans. The changes amounted to a reform of the banking system that forced the industrialists to rely almost entirely on government credit, thereby giving the government new power over the economy. Beneduce, who believed that the state must direct economic growth by using financial inducements rather than by assuming direct responsibility for the regulation of production, scored an important victory.

Having taken IRI out of the lending business, Beneduce concentrated on using the Institute to encourage the reorganization and rationalization of the industries under its control. A preliminary step in that direction was taken in June 1937 when the government put an end to IRI's character as a temporary agency by giving it permanent status as a branch of the public administration. IRI's transformation into a permanent government agency was not popular in business circles but no one contested it strongly. The industrialists could have prevented the change only by buying back the government's vast industrial holdings but they lacked the financial resources to undertake such a major operation. Their failure even to make the attempt has been severely but perhaps unrealistically criticized by disappointed economic liberals who still regret the demise of private initiative in important sectors of the economy.[12]

Private business bought back only those government holdings that promised to be financially attractive (mainly in textiles and in

---

[12] De Stefani, *Baraonda bancaria*, pp. 567–571.

the electrical sector), leaving IRI in control of all those industries that could not operate profitably. That left IRI with a controlling interest in steel, machinery, shipping, electricity, and telephones, with majority margins that ran from 50.6 percent in steel to 99.9 percent in machinery. It was not exactly nationalization because private and public capital remained involved in these sectors, with private capital holding fewer shares. To make matters more complicated, IRI and its affiliates issued their own stock which could be purchased by private investors, a device that not only gave private capital an interest in the preservation of public enterprise but also enabled IRI to raise its own investment capital without having to turn to the government. The arrangement was extremely intricate and novel because it was impossible to tell exactly where private enterprise ended and public enterprise began and because for the first time the coexistence of private and public enterprise within the same economic system was institutionalized and sanctioned by law.

Private industry did not fare badly in this mixed economy. Some industries, particularly textiles, automobiles, and chemicals, remained almost completely in private hands. Even in the publicly owned sectors, the old entrepreneurs and managers remained in charge of production. The market was still controlled by private industrial cartels. In Guarneri's words, government intervention during the Fascist period never went beyond "suggesting a few names for the various boards of directors, usually names of former ambassadors, high-placed civil servants, and, occasionally, of retired party officials being sent to pasture." [13]

If we take the long view, there can be no doubt that IRI has been a boon to private industry. It relieved private capital of all responsibility for its unprofitable commitments and left it free to concentrate on the development of profitable investments. Beneduce's notion that the government should encourage the modernization and expansion of production by indirect means meant that IRI would concentrate on building the infrastructures needed for economic growth. The Italian "economic miracle" that followed the Second World War is probably as much the result of IRI's presence and methods as it is of such developments as the European

---

[13] Guarneri, *Battaglie economiche*, I, 317.

Common Market, foreign investments, and the rise in domestic consumption. It could even be argued that IRI's reluctance to assume direct managerial responsibilities was the only realistic course of action possible in a society that lacked the tradition and expertise for centralized economic planning.[14]

None of IRI's future contributions to economic growth were envisaged by the industrialists during the Fascist period. They accepted public enterprise as an unavoidable necessity. As the government was committed to it for economic and, as we shall see, political reasons, they did not openly criticize the principle of economic interventionism. They tried to restrict the scope of government intervention as much as possible, to retain maximum autonomy and to create the impression that private industry was essentially self-sustaining. Those industries that were still under the control of private capital seemed to be fearful of competition from government subsidized establishments. The chemical industry, for instance, brought this problem to the government's attention soon after the founding of IRI. In spite of private industry's desire to keep public enterprise within the narrowest limits possible, by 1940 the government had a controlling interest in business corporations whose assets represented 17.8 percent of the capital investments in the country and had a minority interest in many others.[15]

Private industry was probably protected from an even greater expansion of public enterprise by the absence of strong economic incentives for the rationalization and expansion of production. The limited national market, the low-level domestic consumption, and the decline in international trade limited the possibilities of modernization in the public and private sectors. Under these circumstances, the fact that government controlled enterprises had access to government funds that were not available to privately owned firms meant relatively little. The one major attempt to rationalize

---

[14] For some ground breaking and essentially positive comments on IRI's economic role, see Pasquale Saraceno, *Lo sviluppo economico dei paesi sovrapopolati* (Rome: Stadium, 1952), pp. 127–137. IRI's contributions to Italian economic development since World War II are emphasized in M. V. Posner and S. J. Woolf, *Italian Public Enterprise* (Cambridge: Harvard University Press, 1967), pp. 58–70.

[15] *O. I.,* June 15, 1933, p. 357. Also, Romeo, *Breve storia della grande industria in Italia,* pp. 169–170.

production in the public sector occurred in the steel industry after 1937 when IRI tried to implement a plan worked out by the industrial engineer Oscar Sinigaglia to concentrate production in a few large plants capable of using the most up-to-date labor saving techniques. The attempt ran into serious difficulties and was not fully carried out until after World War II.[16] The test of strength between public and private enterprise could take place only in an open, dynamic, and less regimented economy. During the Fascist period, even the least efficient firms were protected by the economic regimentation and sluggishness that guaranteed every established producer his share of the market.

In spite of its obvious limitations, IRI represents the closest that fascism ever came to creating that post-capitalist economic order that it promised to achieve through its syndical and corporative reforms. Granted that IRI posed no immediate threat to the survival of private initiative, it was still something new and without counterpart in other countries. Every society that experienced the economic depression witnessed an increase in public regulation of business in the form of subsidies and price controls but it was only in Italy that public and private initiative became intimately and permanently linked by means of institutional innovations. IRI gave the government a control over the economy that was unequalled outside the Soviet Union.

The government tried to use that control in the pursuit of its political objectives. Political considerations account in large measure for the consolidation of public enterprise. The government decree of June 1937, which conferred permanent status upon IRI, specified that IRI could obtain control of privately owned firms whenever it was in the interest of "national defense, the policy of autarky, and the development of the Empire." IRI was in fact authorized to obtain a controlling interest in all privately owned major ship-building firms, a decision that was probably related to the increasing probability of a naval showdown with Great Britain.[17] The expansion and increasing economic importance of the

---

[16] On the Sinigaglia plan, see Bruno Caizzi, *Storia dell'industria italiana dal XVIII secolo ai giorni nostri* (Turin: Unione Tipografico-Editrice Torinese, 1965), pp. 523–527.

[17] *O. I.*, April 22, 1937, p. 7. Also, Guarneri, *Battaglie economiche*, I, 314.

public sector after 1937 were a direct result of the government's expanding military and political commitments. The industrialists had to cope with the domestic repercussions of an expansionist foreign policy.

INDUSTRIAL REACTIONS TO POLITICAL EXPANSIONISM

Guarneri's observation that in politics the industrialists reacted rather than initiated applies more to foreign than to domestic affairs.[18] All available evidence indicates that the major foreign policy decisions in the 1930's, including the war against Ethiopia, the alliance with Germany, military intervention in the Spanish Civil War and World War II, were made by Mussolini and his close political advisers without encouragement from outsiders.

The fact that the industrial leadership played no noticeable role in these decisions does not mean that industry did not benefit from the government's policy of rearmament and territorial expansion. Production and profits increased considerably after 1935 when the country was in a state of continual military mobilization, although it should be remembered that in many industries production and profits began rise as early as 1932-1933. Regardless of what the industrial leaders thought of Mussolini's foreign policy, industrial firms and cartels were eager to seize all opportunities for economic expansion abroad. The CGII organized industrial cartels to develop Ethiopian natural resources soon after the fall of Addis Ababa in May 1936. Within months, approximately 800 Italian firms organized in seventeen cartels operated in Ethiopia amid rumors of widespread profiteering. When Mussolini decided to intervene in the Spanish Civil War, the CGII welcomed the decision as a necessary measure to protect Italian investments in Spain.[19]

---

[18] *Ibid.*, I, 56–57.

[19] Enzo Santarelli, *Storia del movimento e del regime fascista* (Rome: Editori Riuniti, 1967) II, 165–167, 212–219. For a description of the industrial cartels operating in Ethiopia, see Giuseppe Volpi, "L'industria per l'impero," *Rassegna Italiana*, XLVI (October–November 1937), 157–166. The CGII reacted sharply to rumors of corruption and discrimination against labor in Ethiopia. See *O. I.*, October 8, 1936, p. 1; October 22, 1936, p. 1. On the frantic reaction of industry to the threat of a Communist victory in Spain, see *O. I.*, September 3, 1936, p. 1.

Willing as they were to profit from Mussolini's adventures abroad, the industrialists were more preoccupied with the immediate domestic repercussions of an aggressive foreign policy. That preoccupation reveals how different their approach to questions of foreign policy was from Mussolini's. Mussolini played the game of international power politics as if it bore no relationship to the economic realities of the domestic situation. Perhaps he had become the victim of his own propaganda and really believed that his diplomatic genius would compensate for the country's economic vulnerability. Perhaps he took seriously his own assertions that material deprivations would turn the Italian people into a race of heroes. Whatever the explanation, he behaved as if power was more a matter of élan than of economic and military muscle.

The industrialists, on the other hand, were mainly interested in the domestic repercussions of foreign policy decisions. An aggressive foreign policy threatened to create serious business dislocations by disrupting normal trade relations, cutting into the reserves of foreign currencies and precious metals that protected the stability of the lira, and giving government bureaucrats new opportunities to meddle with and extend their control over production. Much of the CGII's work after 1935 had to do with mitigating the impact of war-related government demands on business. Not even the most probusiness government could avoid making new and sometimes burdensome demands. There was a pressing need for additional revenue that meant more and higher taxes. Above all, the government had to think of public opinion which would have reacted unfavorably to continuing preferential treatment for business at a time when people from all walks were being asked to accept heavy financial sacrifices, material deprivations, and to risk their lives in the service of their country.

The government began to increase the pressure on business in September 1935, shortly before the start of actual military operations in Ethiopia, by imposing a six percent ceiling on distributed dividends that was intended to encourage the investment of undistributed profits. At the same time, the government also prohibited corporate capital expansions in excess of one million lire without previous authorization for the purpose of regulating the direction of private investments. The CGII could not openly criticize the adoption of these and other measures without exposing itself to the charge of being more interested in private gain than in the welfare of the nation. It did, however, make it clear that excessive regimentation of production was self-defeating in that it thwarted the industrialists' spontaneous efforts to expand production, a laissez-faire argument that had the great advantage of outwardly reconciling private interest and national needs. The ceiling on dividends was finally lifted in October 1936 but, in its place, the government introduced a progressive tax on distributed dividends and a tax on real property. To make matters even worse for business, the government decided to enact more stringent price controls.[20]

Of all the new taxes on business, none was more resented by the industrialists than the 10 percent levy on the total capital assets of business corporations that was introduced in October 1937. In Pirelli's words, the adoption of this tax was greeted in some quarters with the comment that "the hour of the business corporation had struck." Although Pirelli recognized that the Ministry of Finance applied the tax rather leniently, the industrialists resented even its presence on the books. Their efforts to have the tax repealed were repeatedly frustrated.[21]

The CGII was not always unsuccessful. The burden of taxation on business was often mitigated through administrative channels. Compensations were forthcoming in other forms. The 41 percent devaluation of the lira in October 1936 proved to be a tremendous boon to exporters who found that the new exchange rate made their goods more competitive abroad. Although the needs of business still carried great weight in Mussolini's thinking, the

---

[20] Gino Olivetti, "L'imposta straordinaria sui dividendi," *Riv. Pol. Econ.*, XVII (January 1937), 1–7. Also, *O. I.*, January 30, 1936, pp. 2, 5–6. The restriction on capital expansions was never lifted. The government used it to authorize stock issues by selected firms, including Ansaldo, Ilva, Montecatini, Pirelli, Snia Viscosa, and the *Società Anonima Adriatica di Elettricità*. See ASIA, *Sguardo alla attività dell'Associazione fra le Società Italiane per Azioni nel triennio 1939–1941* (Rome: Cooperativa Tipografica Castaldi, 1941), pp. 150–152.

[21] *O. I.*, October 21, 1937, p. 1; December 30, 1937, p. 8; April 20, 1939, p. 1.

dictator's attitude was changing in ways the industrialists found most disconcerting. International politics now attracted most of his attention. His international prestige and stature as the dean of Fascist dictators gratified his vanity and made him extremely intolerant of anyone who did not share his sense of adventure. His irritation reached a peak when, on his trip back from the famous Munich conference of September 1938 where he was generally credited with having prevented war between the major European powers, he was greeted with triumphal receptions that clearly indicated his countrymen's desire for peace. The industrialists were also exhilarated with Mussolini's performance as a peacemaker and took the opportunity to publicize their wish for a relaxation of international tensions. Their paper *L'Organizzazione Industriale* featured an unusually large banner headline that read: "The *Duce* Has Saved World Peace." [22]

Mussolini did not want recognition as a man of peace when Hitler, whom he had, until then, considered his junior partner, made headlines and scored impressive political triumphs by threatening to make war. He vented his pent-up anger in a confidential speech to party leaders (instructing them to divulge his message by word of mouth) which began with the dramatic assertion that he looked upon the peace-loving, pleasure-seeking *borghesia* (bourgeoisie) as the regime's most dangerous internal enemy.[23] Although he went on to explain that to him the term *borghesia* described a state of mind rather than any particular social group, the message was clear enough: he would pursue his course in foreign policy regardless of how much his critics at home might object.

A few industrialists cautiously expressed their dissatisfaction by continuing to bring attention to the harmful economic and financial repercussions of Mussolini's foreign policy. Pirelli complained before the ASIA general assembly that excessive government interference with business operations hurt the economy. When the great powers went to war in September 1939, the CGII stressed the economic and commercial advantages of Italian neutrality. It changed its tune only after Great Britain indicated, in March 1940, that it

---

[22] *O. I.*, September 30, 1938, p. 1.
[23] *Opera Omnia*, XXIX, 187.

intended to establish a blockade on Italian shipping to Germany.[24]

The objections to British interference with the trade to Germany were not motivated by love of the Germans. The industrialists lived in perpetual fear of the economic might of German industry. As far as the industrialists were concerned, the alliance with Germany was the most objectionable feature of Mussolini's foreign policy. They had appealed to Mussolini as late as February 1935 to protect the domestic market against the influx of German manufactured products, particularly chemicals.[25] At that time, Mussolini still cooperated with France and Great Britain to contain German expansion (the anti-German Stresa agreement was concluded between the three countries in April 1935) and he was glad to oblige the industrialists.

All that changed as a result of the Ethiopian war. As Hitler understood so well, the split between Italy and the western democracies that developed as a result of the Italian attack on Ethiopia left Mussolini no choice but to turn to Germany in order to avoid diplomatic isolation. The political rapprochement between the two countries inevitably entailed a reversal of the anti-German commercial policy and a tightening of economic relations. Conforming to the new political course, delegations of German and Italian industrialists exchanged courtesy visits sponsored by the CGII and its German counterpart, the *Reichsgruppe Industrie*.[26]

Both sides made all the prescribed gestures of friendship and good will to disguise the existence of serious conflicts of interest. When an Italian economic delegation visited Germany in April 1938 to settle the question of Italian economic interests in Austria after the German annexation, a member of the Italian delegation commented that the Germans seemed to be "intoxicated by their own success and consider us all defeated, us a little less defeated than the Austrians but defeated nevertheless."[27] The German an-

---

[24] *O. I.*, April 20, 1939, p. 2; September 12, 1939, p. 1; September 29, 1939, p. 1. Also, Guarneri, *Battaglie economiche*, II, 429–430, 441–446.

[25] *Il Sole*, February 10, 1935, p. 1; February 17, 1935, pp. 1–2; February 18, 1935, p. 1; February 21, 1935, pp. 4–5; February 24, 1935, pp. 3–4.

[26] *O. I.*, October 22, 1936, p. 1; April 8, 1937, p. 7; May 6, 1937, p. 1; May 6, 1938, p. 1; June 24, 1938, p. 1.

[27] Guarneri, *Battaglie economiche,* II, 305.

nexation of Austria proved to be a troublesome development for Italian industry. The industrialists had the satisfaction of seeing the preferential tariffs that had facilitated the importation of Austrian manufactured products abolished but they lost access to important markets and sources of raw materials. The annexation of Austria gave the Germans complete control of the railroads connecting the port of Trieste to central and northern Europe. The Germans took advantage of their control of transportation to divert traffic from Trieste to their own ports, particularly Hamburg, by fixing their railroad rates so that they discriminated against traffic originating from Italy. German industry also arrogated to itself quantities of Austrian coal, steel, and lumber that had previously gone to Italy. Finally, the annexation of Austria gave German exporters a better vantage point to penetrate the Balkan markets that were still dominated by Italy.

Germany's behavior after the annexation of Austria confirmed the suspicions of many Italian industrialists that Germany wanted to transform Italy into an agrarian client state. German experts argued the point openly in the cold language and logic of economics. They were astonishingly candid considering how sensitive Italian industrialists were on that score. Encouraged perhaps by polite statements from CGII officials to the effect that the Italian and German economies were complementary, Walther Funk, Germany's economic commissioner, told a shocked Guarneri in January 1939 that it would be economically advantageous for both countries to agree to a division of functions whereby Italy would specialize in agriculture and Germany in manufacturing.[28]

Funk's tactless remarks suggested that if the Germans had their way they would not hesitate to suffocate Italian industry. After that, Italian industrial leaders were less polite toward their German comrades. Volpi told a group of German visitors in June 1939 that the Italian and German economies were not, after all, entirely complementary. Guarneri took it upon himself as minister for foreign trade and currency exchanges to make it clear to the Germans that Italian producers were not prepared to become their economic vassals. He expressed his annoyance and that of many industrialists by curtailing Italian exports of manpower, aluminum

---

[28] *Ibid.*, II, 312–313, 319–333.

products, agricultural foodstuffs, mercury, sulphur, and rayon to Germany in retaliation for the Germans' hesitancy in honoring balance of payments credits to Italy.[29]

These verbal and commercial skirmishes reveal the industrialists' fear of Germany because they occurred at the time when the Italian and German governments were in the process of concluding the famous Pact of Steel of May 1939. The timing suggests that the industrialists were trying to apply the brakes at the moment Mussolini committed the country to an unqualified political and military alliance with Germany. If that was indeed their intention, they did not succeed. Mussolini continued to behave as if considerations of economic convenience were irrelevant. His decision to enter World War II on Germany's side in June 1940 was essentially a political gamble probably motivated by his conviction that a complete German victory was imminent and that he must hasten to make a show of force in order to participate in the peace settlement.

By that time, many industrialists seemed to be equally mesmerized by Germany's military victories. In a book published in June 1940, Pirelli argued that the Axis powers were sure to win because German *Blitzkrieg* tactics eliminated the possibility of a long war of attrition that would have given the enemy the opportunity to utilize his superior economic resources.[30] Faced by the prospect of a rapid German victory, industrial leaders were torn between their fear of Germany's suspected designs on the Italian economy and their eagerness to take advantage of the opportunities for economic expansion abroad that would follow a joint German-Italian victory. Mussolini still believed Italy could avoid German domination by waging its own "parallel war" as Germany's equal partner and some industrialists apparently shared the belief. Volpi wrote in September 1940 that the CGII and the *Reichsgruppe Industrie* were planning for the economic reconstruction of Europe after a Fascist victory.[31]

---

[29] *Ibid.*, II, 317–319. Also, *O. I.*, June 27, 1939, p. 2.

[30] Alberto Pirelli, *Economia e guerra* (Milan: Istituto per gli Studi di Politica Internazionale, 1940), I, 7–8. The industrialists' unquestioning faith in Germany's industrial and military power was also noticed at the time by the diplomat Raffaele Guariglia, *Ricordi, 1922–1946* (Naples: Edizioni Scientifiche Italiane, 1949), pp. 442–443.

[31] Giuseppe Volpi, "L'economia di domani," *Riv. Pol. Econ.*, XXX (September–October 1940), 625–626.

As the prospects of victory diminished and Italy became more dependent on German economic and military support, both Mussolini and the industrialists realized how seriously they had miscalculated. Because Mussolini found it impossible to separate himself from Hitler, the industrialists had to separate themselves from both. The fall of Mussolini's government on July 25, 1943 and the announcement of September 8 that General Pietro Badoglio's government had signed an armistice with the Allies gave the industrial leaders a chance to begin severing their relationship with fascism. Although they were inhibited by the fact that Mussolini and the Germans were not dislodged from Northern Italy—where most industrial plants were located—until the end of the war, after 1943 the Fascist and the industrial leadership drifted apart. In a futile effort to gain popularity with the workers, Mussolini decided in February 1944 that all industrial enterprises with assets of more than one million lire were to be nationalized and that freely elected workers' representatives were to sit on the boards of directors of both the nationalized and privately owned firms. Mussolini justified these steps to the German ambassador who questioned their advisability by pointing out that "many leaders of Italian industry are awaiting the Anglo-Saxons with open arms and in great part are responsible for the treachery of September 8." [32]

That last-minute comeback of Fascist radicalism would be entirely irrelevant were it not for the fact that it draws attention to the revolutionary aspirations that had always been latent in fascism. For twenty years the industrialists had frustrated those aspirations. The industrialists had never been strong enough to dominate fascism but they had been sufficiently influential to protect their business interests. As long as Mussolini needed an Italian basis of power, he could not afford to ignore their demands. Similarly, the more he had to rely on Germany, the freer he was of his domestic supporters—big business and the monarchy—whose influence had restrained the more radical Fascist currents in the past. It is not surprising that Mussolini fell back on the more radical aspirations of fascism once he was little more than a German puppet. At that point in his political career he had to use what remained of his

---

[32] Quoted in F. W. Deakin, *The Brutal Friendship. Mussolini, Hitler, and the Fall of Italian Fascism* (New York: Harper and Row, 1962), p. 670.

talent for compromise and political maneuvering to deal with the Germans. He could afford to be rigid with the industrialists because, politically, they no longer had anything to offer him.

Conversely, he had nothing to offer to them. The relationship that had been an asset in the past was now a serious liability. The industrialists, who liked to place their bets on the winning horse, looked around for a more attractive ally. Italian big business was rescued from its entanglements with fascism and from the danger of economic suffocation at the hands of Germany by the military victory of the capitalist democracies. To explore that question we would have to look closer at the relationship between the industrial and the Fascist leaderships during World War II. Such a study would hinge on the theme of increasing alienation while ours revolves around that of gradual engagement and partnership.

CONCLUSION

THE BALANCE SHEET BEFORE
THE CATASTROPHE OF WAR

Fascism aspired to become a melting pot for the most diverse interests and ideas. Instead, if the analogy may be allowed, it was more like an inefficient pressure cooker that softens but cannot change its contents into a homogeneous whole. As Antonio Gramsci observed in 1926, when the Fascist regime reached out to absorb all of Italian society it absorbed all of society's tensions and conflicts.[1] Under fascism, the conflicts were muted or repressed but never eradicated.

In trying to compose social conflicts, fascism followed the line of least resistance. Instead of insisting that the various interest groups submit to the will of the Fascist leadership (assuming that a leadership as diverse as the Fascist could agree to any specific course of action), Mussolini found it more expedient to bargain for the support of every interest group that was willing to cooperate with fascism. He reserved the forceful approach for the groups, par-

---

[1] From Gramsci's speech to the Third Congress of the Communist Party of Italy, January 1926, quoted in De Felice, *Mussolini il fascista,* II, 4. On Gramsci's analysis of fascism, see also Cammett, *Antonio Gramsci and the Origins of Italian Communism,* p. 179.

ticularly industrial workers, who put up stiff resistance. All other groups received adequate compensation for services rendered. What each interest group gained in return for its support depended, of course, on its bargaining power and political leverage.

Had fascism been the monolithic, unyielding force that it claimed to be, it might never have come to power. The presence within its ranks of the most diverse groups and ideas was in effect fascism's strongest political asset on the way to power (once in power, that diversity became a liability because it precluded consensus and clarity of purpose). Internal heterogeneity attracted support from the most varied external sources. Business leaders, old-style liberal politicians, the army, the Church, the monarchy, and various other groups found it possible to identify with fascism in varying degrees because they saw within it groups and ideas that they found congenial. They accepted a dialogue with fascism because they assumed that it would be sympathetic to their particular needs. In this study we examined one of the dialogues. On the basis of what we have seen, we conclude that fascism's most striking characteristic was its readiness to compromise. Studies of other dialogues and compromises indicate that the Fascist practice of government was as flexible and accommodating as its concept of leadership was rigid and unyielding.[2]

But to argue that fascism was flexible is not to suggest that it surrendered to the demands of its supporters. To argue that point would be as misleading as to argue that we should take the totalitarian aspirations of fascism at their face value. We must resist the proposition of mechanical leader-follower relationships of either kind. To understand the reality of Fascist experience in Italy we must abandon the concept of absolute unilateral power for that of reciprocal influence.

All outside groups who rallied to fascism in the hope of manipulating it in their interest discovered sooner or later that they had

---

[2] On the army, see Giorgio Rochat, *L'esercito italiano da Vittorio Veneto a Mussolini (1919–1925)* (Bari: Laterza, 1967), pp. 408–448. On the Church, see Francesco Margiotta Broglio, *Italia e Santa Sede dalla grande guerra alla conciliazione. Aspetti politici e giuridici* (Bari: Laterza, 1966), pp. 249–257. We are still lacking a good study of the relationship between the monarchy and fascism. Some interesting material appears in Nino D'Aroma, *Vent'anni insieme. Vittorio Emanuele e Mussolini* (Rocca San Casciano: Cappelli, 1957).

miscalculated. Some groups miscalculated greatly, others only a little. The old liberal politicians miscalculated most because they were completely replaced by a new political leadership of lower middle class parvenus who would not have risen as high through the old electoral and parliamentary channels. The prerogatives of the monarchy diminished to the point that fascism asserted even its right to interfere with the succession to the throne. The army had to accept the presence of a rival paramilitary organization, the Fascist Militia. The Church could not prevent fascism from gaining almost complete control of education. We may well quote the mocking words from the final chorus in Giuseppe Verdi's *Falstaff: tutti gabbati.*

Where do we place the industrial leadership along this continuum of combined submission and resistance? Unquestionably among the groups who yielded the least and gained the most. The limits of their power were real enough but were not of a nature to seriously jeopardize what they most prized, their control of production. The industrialists' first gain in order of time was also their most significant in the long run. The March on Rome ended their state of psychological insecurity resulting from the freedom enjoyed under liberal governments by political parties and labor organizations hostile to capitalism. Fascist radicals who were also hostile to business did not have the kind of strong popular support that made their Socialist rivals so powerful within the factories. Fascism's rise to power created the authoritarian climate that the industrialists needed to run their factories without having to worry about interference from workers who wanted a voice in management or liberal governments that were responsive to popular pressures.

There were other lasting gains for the industrialists. The laissez-faire policy followed by the Fascist government from 1922 to 1925 gave them the freedom of action that they needed to take full advantage of new business opportunities that were due to the general expansion of production and trade typical of those prosperous years. Fascism gave Italian businessmen the normalcy that businessmen in the United States enjoyed without having to back insurrectionary movements. The syndical reform of 1925 entailed a rejection of the principle but not usually of the practice of laissez-faire.

In return for the government's rejection of the laissez-faire ideal, the industrial leaders gained more effective control over individual employers and greater influence over the public administration. During the economic depression of the 1930's, the restrictions to private initiative gave established producers an unique opportunity to eliminate the last vestiges of competition and entrench themselves on the national market.

On the debit side of the industrialists' balance sheet, we must list the loss of private status by business associations. While the change was really felt in agriculture, banking, and commerce, it was only a minor inconvenience in industry. The CGII and its affiliates continued to choose their own officials and to enjoy *de facto* autonomy. Nevertheless, some industrialists feared that the transformation of private business associations into extensions of the government bureaucracy was the first step toward complete regulation of private initiative by the government.

Subsequent developments did nothing to allay the fears. Mussolini's stubborn defense of *quota 90* in 1927 was the first major sign that the Fascist leadership would not allow economic considerations to obstruct political goals. The industrialists were understandably concerned when that thinking became the norm in the late 1930's rather than the exception as it had been earlier. Political considerations led to the consolidation of public enterprise and to the alliance with Germany. The industrialists' objections to Fascist foreign policy were not grounded in moral scruples against aggression and war. The industrialists only feared the possible loss of their political influence and economic privileges.

A comparison of the debits and credits shows that the credits were of a tangible nature, while most debits were in the form of preoccupations about the future. The industrialists had to be on guard against what fascism might become rather than against what it actually was. Their awareness of the presence in fascism of hostile elements and dangerous ideas is what enabled them to minimize their losses. They did well because they never took the benevolence of fascism for granted. Their suspicion indicates that they understood the nature of fascism better than those who equated it with blind social reaction.

The industrialists were not strong enough to dominate fascism but were sufficiently influential to thwart the plans of self-styled Fascist social revolutionaries. Public enterprise became a reality, but in diluted form that left room for private initiative. Taxes and bureaucratic controls on business increased, but the industrialists were able to mitigate their impact on production by administrative recourse. If we consider what actually happened rather than what might have been, the partnership with fascism was a profitable business venture for the industrialists. Their strongest asset in dealing with fascism was that they knew exactly what they wanted whereas the Fascists pursued too many vague and conflicting goals. It is sometimes more advantageous to have the narrow vision and persistence of the hedgehog than the sly virtuosity of the fox.

EPILOGUE

Reminders of the Fascist past are not conspicuous in Italy today. The casual visitor may travel the length of the peninsula without noticing anything more striking than an occasional fading Fascist inscription on a dilapidated roadside building. The obelisk in honor of the *Duce* that still stands proudly at the periphery of downtown Rome is a rare memento. The inconspicuousness is easily explained. In their understandable eagerness to forget the Fascist past, the Italian people did a rather thorough job of eliminating its most visible reminders soon after the fall of the regime. There is no room in the life style of the contemporary Italian for the values of the Fascist ethic. Gone is the "heroic" pose that manifested itself in a profusion of military uniforms, the well-staged mass rallies, the seemingly endless lines of marching troops, and the xenophobia of Fascist propaganda. The antimaterialist bias of fascism is forgotten (it was probably never taken seriously) as Italians in increasing numbers eagerly seize every available opportunity to satisfy long repressed material wants. Nationalism and militarism are dirty words, particularly among the generation born after 1940.

Yet, in spite of the obvious differences between contemporary and Fascist Italy, the legacy of fascism is still present. It becomes noticeable as soon as we look beneath the surface. At the level of physical evidence, the knowledgeable observer will recognize the Fascist touch in the architecture of many public buildings which reveals how the Fascist mind was torn between functionalism and rhetoric. The Fascist imprint can be seen at its most spectacular in the grand sweep of Mussolini's *Via dell'Impero* which winds its way among the ruins of ancient Rome in the center of the city; it is recognizable in the geometric layout of a model town, or in the neat lines of a farm house that was built as part of a Fascist land reclamation project.

The legacy of fascism is strongest where it can neither be seen nor touched. To argue this point is perhaps to question the widely accepted view that fascism is a closed parenthesis in Italian history. It is difficult to identify the elements of continuity that connect fascism to the past and the present. The concept of *trasformismo,* first used by the political analyst Guido Dorso to place fascism in the context of Italian history, is particularly useful for our purpose because it points to the uniform ways in which power is exercized by different governments under cover of changing ideological formulas. This particular approach to fascism indicates that the Fascist regime intensified and passed on some undesirable traits of public life.

The term *trasformismo* describes a tendency to sacrifice political coherence for the sake of expediency, indicates the absence of well-defined political programs, and points to the prevalence of governments that rely on makeshift coalitions of special interest groups. Such governments rarely have the freedom of action to confront the most fundamental problems of society. By practicing *trasformismo* and attempting at the same time to disguise the fact under the trappings of a totalitarian state, fascism ultimately lessened public respect for government. Popular faith in political leaders, never strong in Italy, was further weakened. That faith is more tenuous today than it has ever been. Without attempting to minimize the shortcomings of today's political leadership, the fact remains that the widespread tendency to assume that every politician is a crook becomes in itself a powerful obstacle to reform.

An inadequate sense of civic responsibility seems to be a particularly harmful aspect of the legacy of fascism. Although a number of Fascist leaders, most notably Dino Grandi, argued early in their careers that it was the historical function of fascism to bridge the gap between rulers and ruled, the example set by the Fascist leadership did little to transform the individual into the citizen. It was not the frank elitism of Fascist thought that alienated many Italians, rather, it was the gap between promise and achievement. To survive politically, a public figure had to operate on two levels. Outwardly, he had to behave like a disciplined member of the Fascist party. Behind the scenes, he had to be a devious political maneuverer. Not everyone could meet both requirements. For Mussolini the double standard was a psychological necessity. The dictatorial pose gratified his immense ego while the hidden power game appealed to the backstairs politician in him. Others, and most business leaders fall in this category, accepted the rules of the game because they were essentially indifferent to the constitutional and moral implications of their political actions. They looked upon politics as a waste of their valuable time; the only abstraction they understood and appreciated was that business is business. For a few, the political atmosphere of Fascist Italy was unbearable. Proud and lonely figures like Gaetano Salvemini and Count Carlo Sforza who attached great importance to moral integrity or personal dignity preferred exile to compliance. Not that all Fascist leaders were unprincipled opportunists; there were among them sincere reformers who tried to unite the regime and the masses in ways more lasting than those of demagogy. Their gravest error was that they kept hoping long after it should have been perfectly clear that theirs was an impossible task.

The behavior of the Fascist leadership reinforced the old popular suspicion that political power is for the benefit of the powerful few. But the adverse legacy of fascism is apparent in other ways, too. Popular distrust of public officials was intensified when fascism proceeded to expand the role of the bureaucracy in Italian life. The strong authoritarianism that radiates from the bureaucracy is still a fact of everyday life in Italy. Although the cult of *libro e moschetto* (book and rifle) is a thing of the past, the authoritarian bias is still present in Italian education. And because it was not removed by public action, it is now challenged in the streets by rioting students.

The individualism of the average Italian is probably reenforced by the general awareness of how difficult it is to become a participating member of the community. If the individual cannot identify with the officials who wield public power, then he must rely on himself and on those to whom he is related by family ties. At most, he may identify with the immediate community of village or town. Anyone familiar with the Italian scene knows how strong municipal loyalties still are. Beyond these familiar spheres, the individual knows that he encounters the alien domain of officialdom, a *terra incognita* to be entered only in case of necessity and with the greatest circumspection. To this day, many Italians will venture into that strange land only after they have assured themselves that the encounter with the bureaucrat will take place on personal grounds. Every Italian understands the importance of the spoken or written introduction, the *raccomandazione* that is designed to create a man-to-man relationship between the citizen and the public official.

Lack of faith in official channels of communication is evident in the behavior of pressure groups. The apparent irrelevance of political programs encourages organized interests to approach the decision-makers through channels of their own making. Through such channels decisions of public interest are made without adequate public discussion. Questions that require the attention of responsible government officials are often left to the discretion of bureaucratic bodies. Far from being an unfortunate by-product of the system, the pervasive bureaucracy has become a necessary part of the political process. When the Italian bureaucracy is given explicit instructions, it is capable of carrying them out promptly and efficiently. When it is left without guidance, it inevitably flounders because it reflects the indecisiveness in the political process.

Under these circumstances, private interests find it particularly advantageous to establish their own preserves in the public administration. We have seen how the industrialists influenced the administration under fascism. The dismantling of the corporative state left them temporarily disconcerted but they were quick to repair the damage. The Ministry of Industry and Commerce, the direct descendant of the old Ministry of Corporations, is today probably more solicitous of CGII interests than the Ministry of Corporations ever was. Even in parliament where opposition to the CGII is strongest, the industrialists have been able to play an important role by controlling the small but well-endowed and articulate Liberal party. Liberal support enabled Prime Minister Alcide De Gasperi to govern without having to rely on Socialist or Communist votes in parliament after 1947. The Liberal party's laissez-faire philosophy guided public policy in the crucial period of economic reconstruction after World War II.

Continuing a pattern already evident during the Fascist period, since 1945 the industrialists have not consistently advocated economic laissez-faire. They have not allowed their reverence for the laissez-faire doctrine to interfere with their pursuit of economically expedient goals. Their rejection of communism on ideological grounds has not prevented businessmen from trading and investing in Communist countries. Nor have they objected, except perhaps in specific cases, to the expansion of public enterprise at home. Business leaders were quick to learn that in the postwar economy the private sector could actually benefit from economic interventionism. By relieving the private sector of financial responsibility for the branches of production that could not operate profitably in the international economy of the postwar period, the government enabled private business to concentrate on the development of the sectors of production that are strong enough to withstand competition from abroad. Private business has thus been able to take advantage of the unprecedented economic opportunities of the European Common Market. Therefore, the consolidation of public enterprise has made it possible for businessmen successfully to face the challenges of an open international economy that would have been ruinous for them at any other time in history.

Other challenges of an open society may not be so easily coped with. There is the threat of an aggressive labor movement that has recently generated the kind of intense social unrest that prevailed in Italy after the First World War. Until recently, the industrialists were able to contain the pressure of organized labor by making significant concessions to privileged groups of workers and by exploiting ideological differences that kept the labor movement politically divided. There is evidence that such tactics may not work well in the future. The current wave of strikes in Italy indicates a growing tendency among workers to close ranks regardless of political differences. Young workers seem to be more militant than their labor leaders. Bread-and-butter demands feature prominently among the requests of strikers and these demands threaten to cut deeply into profits.

The prospect of unity of action among the workers poses a serious challenge to the entire society because no one knows how to deal with it. Business, government, and public opinion are all equally unprepared to deal calmly and rationally with agitations that disrupt daily life and inconvenience nearly everyone. It is at this point that the dangerous legacy of fascism may assert itself most threateningly. The passage of time has blunted the memory of the many obnoxious features of life in a regimented society. In many cases, people were probably more disappointed with the corruption and ineptitude of the Fascist regime than with the authoritarian philosophy of fascism. The persistence of authoritarian attitudes explains in part many Italians' contempt toward their present political leadership. The velvet hand is often less appealing than the iron fist.

The most effective cure for the widespread lack of confidence in the political process is probably the steady and prolonged practice of participatory democracy. Unfortunately, participatory democracy can be a painful cure. It is accompanied by disturbing side-effects: strikes, rioting, and government instability. Because the turmoil usually causes acute discomfort to many people, it is all too often perceived as a sign of social decay. Panic reactions are likely to occur in today's highly integrated societies in which the legitimate demands of one group often cannot be satisfied without infringing on the acquired privileges of another. When all legitimate demands for change are put together, they seem to constitute a threat to everything that is familiar and cherished. There is always a strong temptation to repress that threat by force. Perhaps the only people who can see the turmoil as the birth pangs of a better society are the lucky few who are not personally affected.

The danger of repression is particularly endemic to the societies that, by accident or design, have experienced prolonged periods of social calm. In these societies it is often erroneously assumed that the absence of social conflict is a normal condition of life and that the expression of grievances rather than the existence of glaring inequities creates instability. The danger of a neo-Fascist reaction in Italy is probably greater because the Fascist experience fostered illusions. Fascism introduced a period of outward calm by force-fully repressing the aspirations of organized labor, but failed to educate public opinion about the realities of social life in the absence of force.

The danger of future repression is not confined to Italy. Many Americans share the assumption that social consensus is the trademark of a sound society. That belief is particularly ingrained among Americans who remember with nostalgia the placid 1950's. Their attitude resembles that of many older Italians who are perhaps reappraising the Fascist experience in the light of what is happening today. Perhaps fascism is rooted in the longing for nirvana, a longing that sooner or later manifests itself in rapidly changing societies.

Rapid social change is usually accompanied by increasing political polarization. Fascism has been one answer to such polarization. However, before we pin the Fascist label on contemporary movements we should keep in mind that fascism never presented itself as an instrument of social conservatism. Fascist movements have always tried to appeal to a broad cross section of society in a calculated effort to isolate revolutionary extremists. A simple law-and-order platform does not have that broad an appeal. Fascist leaders always emphasized that they approved of legitimate demands for change and that they objected primarily only to the antinational orientation and doctrinaire rigidity of other revolutionary movements. They deliberately cultivated a dynamic image designed to appeal particularly to those members of the younger generations who were eager for change. Fascism persevered in this revolutionary pose even as it courted conservative interests that wanted to minimize social change. The historical novelty of fascism was that it succeeded in that difficult gambit. Most law-and-order movements today do not even attempt it; they are usually little more than aggressive forms of traditional conservatism.

The most surprising thing about fascism is that it managed to retain credibility as a revolutionary movement in the eyes of millions in spite of its most unrevolutionary record in power. That feat would not have been possible without the political shrewdness and demagogic talents of Hitler and Mussolini. No Fascist movement could prolong the interaction of conflicting aspirations in the absence of a charismatic synthesizer like Hitler or Mussolini. There may be leaders today who would like to do what the Fascist dictators did but none seem to have their political imagination. If it is true, however, that leaders are made by circumstances, then the Fascist personality may reappear on the political scene. The panic that is generated in our own society by alarmistic reports on crime, conspiracy, and moral degradation, and by the social repercussions of rapid technological change, may yet play into the hands of talented, ambitious, and unscrupulous politicians. If that should happen, perhaps our awareness of what fascism really was will help us recognize the demon though he appear in the guise of a redeemer.

BIBLIOGRAPHICAL NOTE

No attempt will be made here to list all the primary and secondary sources that have been cited or consulted in conjunction with this study. The reader will find complete references to most of these works in the footnotes. Here we mention only those works that deal explicitly with the relationship between the business and political leaderships in Fascist Italy in the hope that these brief bibliographical comments will indicate how the present study relates to the work done so far by scholars.

The publications issued or sponsored by the ASIA and CGII constitute the largest and most important source of information. This vast material that has never before been studied in its entirety consists of annual reports, periodic summaries of the work done by the various services and bureaus of these two associations, circulars to the membership, trade journals, and scholarly periodicals. Extensive use was also made of publications issued by other business associations and government agencies, parliamentary records, memoirs, and archive collections. With one minor exception, the material from the Tullio Cianetti and Giuseppe Volpi collections in the *Carteggi di Personalità* of the *Archivio Centrale dello Stato* (Rome) is not cited in the footnotes. It is mentioned here because the two collections have provided supplementary evidence that the author used in other studies closely related to this one.

The consulted secondary sources begin with the numerous publications of contemporary observers who expressed views and formulated judgments that have become important and necessary reference points of the current debate on the relationship between the business and political leaderships. Reactions on the Marxist Left varied from cut-and-dried condemnations of fascism as an outgrowth of large-scale industrial capitalism to highly sophisticated analyses of fascism as a form of disguised social reaction. Daniel Guerin's *Fascism and Big Business* (New York: Pioneer Publishers, 1939), first published in French, is a typical example of the more heavy handed identifications of fascism and capitalism. A more subtle correlation between them is drawn in an important work by an anonymous Italian Marxist writing in the Soviet Union in the 1920's, *Il fascismo in Italia. Leningrado 1926. Studio inedito per i quadri dell' Internazionale comunista* (Milan: Edizioni del Gallo, 1965), edited by Renzo De Felice. Still within the Marxist tradition, but reflecting an awareness of the mixed social composition of the Fascist movement, is the classic work by Angelo Tasca (pseud. A. Rossi), *The Rise of Italian Fascism, 1918–1922* (London: Methuen, 1938), best consulted in its Italian edition, *Nascita e avvento del fascismo. L'Italia dal 1918 al 1922* (Florence: La Nuova Italia, 1950).

Gaetano Salvemini's extensive writings on fascism are now being collected in the *Opere di Gaetano Salvemini. Scritti sul fascismo* (3 vols.; Milan: Feltrinelli, 1961 to date), of which only the first two volumes have appeared. Salvemini's writings are difficult to categorize in strictly political terms. They are animated by a strong moral revulsion against fascism and its supporters. Business leaders are not spared by Salvemini but he is too careful an historian to overlook any of the documentary evidence available to him. Hence, his writings often display an awareness that fascism was much more than the armed guard of big business and are extremely rich in factual information. His *Under the Axe of Fascism* (London: Victor Gollanctz, 1936), to be included in the third volume of the *Scritti,* is particularly relevant to our topic.

Of the more detached scholarly studies of fascism written while the regime was still in power, special mention must be made of Louis Rosenstock-Franck's two works, *L'économie corporative fasciste en doctrine et en fait* (Paris: Librairie Universitaire J. Gambier, 1934), and *Les étapes de l'économie fasciste italienne; du corporatisme à l'économie de guerre* (Paris: Librairie Sociale et Economique, 1939). Rosenstock-Franck's analysis of the personnel shared by business and government agencies is as valuable today as it was when it was written. A short work by G. Lowell Field, *The Syndical and Corporative Institutions of Italian Fascism* (New York: Columbia University Press, 1938) is still the most complete and concise guide to the labyrinthine institutional arrangements of the Fascist state that assured organized industry a large margin of independence. Some compromises behind these reforms are discussed in Alberto Aquarone's *L'organizzazione dello Stato totalitario* (Turin: Giulio Einaudi, 1965). The importance of these compromises clearly indicates that the Fascist state was not as totalitarian as the title of Aquarone's book seems to suggest.

An early attempt to assess the impact of the regime's institutional apparatus on the implementation of economic policies is found in William G. Welk, *Fascist Economic Policy* (Cambridge: Harvard University Press, 1938), reprinted by Russell & Russell of New York in 1968. A more recent evaluation appears in Shepard B. Clough, "Il fascismo in Italia: linee della sua politica economica," *Il Nuovo Osservatore,* VI (November–December 1965), 826–833.

Interest in the relationship between fascism and vested economic interests has remained strong since World War II. Of the major postwar studies, the first in order of time is Ernesto Rossi's *I padroni del vapore* (Bari: Laterza, 1955), revised and reissued by the same publisher in 1966 under the title *Padroni del vapore e fascismo.* Rossi carried on in the tradition of Salvemini with scrupulous regard for factual accuracy and pungency of language.

One of the first to challenge the validity of Rossi's approach was the president of the CGII, Dr. Angelo Costa. In the course of a television debate of November 10, 1955, Costa argued that, although Rossi's book contained no noticeable factual errors, it nevertheless conveyed the erroneous impression that the industrialists had been active promoters of the Fascist regime. Costa's argument conformed to the evidence presented by such industrial leaders as Ettore Conti in *Il taccuino di un borghese* (Milan: Garzanti, 1946), and Felice Guarneri in *Battaglie economiche tra le due grandi guerre* (2 vols.; Milan: Garzanti, 1953). These two works are particularly valuable because they contain precious information about industrialists whose views and personalities were always shrouded in mystery.

In the light of this additional evidence, scholars of all political persuasions began to call for a reassessment of the problem that would take into account the conflicting aspirations of Italian fascism. It became clear that the relationship between industry and fascism defied simple, mechanical cause-and-effect explanations. Of particular interest in this respect are the works of Paolo Alatri, especially his bibliographical article "Recenti studi sul fascismo," *Studi Storici*, III (October–December 1962), 757–836, and the essay by Vittorio Foa, "Le strutture economiche e la politica economica del regime fascista," in *Fascismo e antifascismo. Lezioni e testimonianze, 1918–1948* (2 vols.; Milan: Feltrinelli, 1963).

Responding to the need for reassessment, a number of scholars have recently stressed the differences in the outlook of business and Fascist leaders. The desire to challenge the traditional Marxist interpretation of fascism as a political projection of capitalism is evident in Mario Abrate's *La lotta sindacale nella industrializzazione in Italia, 1906–1926* (Turin: Franco Angeli, 1967), in the first three volumes of Renzo De Felice's monumental biography of Mussolini (the only ones published so far), *Mussolini il rivoluzionario, 1883–1920* (Turin: Giulio Einaudi, 1965), *Mussolini il fascista, 1921–1929* (2 vols.; Turin: Giulio Einaudi, 1966–1968), and in Piero Melograni's "Confindustria e fascismo tra il 1919 e il 1925," *Il Nuovo Osservatore*, VI (November–December 1965), 834–873.

As this author has also argued in an article on "Fascism and the Industrial Leadership in Italy Before the March on Rome," *Industrial and Labor Relations Review*, XXI (April 1968), 400–417 (the article has been completely revised and expanded to form Chapter I of this study), business leaders were particularly attracted by the laissez-faire part of the Fascist program. They did not approve of the revolutionary aspirations of fascism and tried their best to neutralize the influence of Fascist radicals within the movement.

Writers on the subject now fall into one or the other of two categories: those who like Abrate, De Felice, and Melograni stress the subjective differences in the outlook of business and Fascist leaders and those who, like Franco Catalano in *Potere economico e fascismo. La crisi del dopoguerra, 1919–1921* (Milan: Lerici, 1964), "Riflessi economico-sociali dello sviluppo dell'industria italiana dall'inizio del novecento," in *Dal quattrocento al novecento* (Milan: La Goliardica, 1966), and in other writings, have their eyes on the objective, tangible gains that business leaders achieved or hoped to achieve by supporting fascism. Until now no one has attempted to show how business interests managed to expand their influence within the Fascist state in spite of the undeniable difference that separated the business and Fascist leaderships. It is hoped that the present study will fill that gap and will give the reader a reasonably clear idea of the extent and limits of the power of private business under fascism.

INDEX

Abrate, Mario, 64, 68n, 149

Agnelli, Giovanni: early organizational activities in industry, 9; early contacts with Fascist leaders, 20, 29; on the workers' occupation of the factories (September 1920), 26; attitude toward government, 40

Alatri, Paolo, 149

Ansaldo enterprises, 20, 109n, 117, 127n

Aquarone, Alberto, 148

Arias, Gino, 87

ASIA (*Associazione fra le Società Italiane per Azioni*) 55, 128; relationship to CGII, 3–4, 11, 12; on Italian intervention in First World War, 10; on elections of April 1924, 64

Badoglio, Pietro, 132

Balbo, Italo, 22, 31

Banca Commerciale Italiana, 119

Banca Italiana di Sconto, 117

Banchelli, Umberto, 21

Banco di Roma, 117

Bank of Italy, 109

Belluzzo, Giuseppe, 49n, 99

Beneduce, Alberto, 119–121, 122

Benni, Antonio Stefano, 6, 7, 14, 34, 35, 37, 38, 47, 49, 83, 105n; on economic protectionism, 54–55, 56n, 104; interest in foreign markets, 57; on Fascist syndicalism, 60–61, 62n, 63, 64, 70–71; on elections of April 1924, 64–65; on Matteotti crisis, 68; on Vidoni Palace agreement, 71–72; objects to compulsory arbitration in labor disputes, 73–74; on corporativism, 95, 97, 98, 99; on cartels, 100; on public enterprise, 118

Bonomi, Ivanoe, 119

Borletti, Senatore, 29

Bottai, Giuseppe (Fascist theoretician and minister of corporations), 69; on relationship between syndicalism and corporativism, 77, 96; activities as minister of corporations, 82, 89; on role of industrial cartels, 99, 101

Buozzi, Bruno, 26

Buronzo, Vincenzo, 85

Capoferri, Pietro (leader of Fascist industrial labor unions), 90, 103n, 109n

Caporetto, battle of, 21

Carli, Filippo, 59